D0079308

TELEPOWER, PLANNING, and SOCIETY

TELEPOWER, PLANNING, and SOCIETY

Crisis in Communication

MELVILLE C. BRANCH

PRAEGER

Westport, Connecticut
London

Library of Congress Cataloging-in-Publication Data

Branch, Melville Campbell.
Telepower, planning, and society : crisis in communication / Melville C. Branch.
p. cm.
Includes bibliographical references and index.
ISBN 0–275–94599–5 (alk. paper)
1. Planning. 2. Mass media. 3. Telecommunication. I. Title.
HD87.5.B733 1994
384′.068—dc20 94–15882

British Library Cataloguing in Publication Data is available.

Library of Congress Catalog Card Number: 94–15882
ISBN: 0–275–94599–5

First published in 1994

Praeger Publishers, 88 Post Road West, Westport, CT 06881
An imprint of Greenwood Publishing Group, Inc.

Printed in the United States of America

The paper used in this book complies with the Permanent Paper Standard issued by the National Information Standards Organization (Z39.48–1984).

10 9 8 7 6 5 4 3 2 1

Contents

Preface

In *Planning: Universal Process* (1990), the author discussed planning as an innate, intuitive, and deliberate process which is inherent in the lives and activities of humans. First as a chemical and later as an intuitive force directing the evolution of animate life over billions of years from a single cellular beginning. And during the past several hundred thousand years as a conscious and deliberate endeavor by humanoids, primitive people, and men and women as they are today. The five and a half billion people on earth today plan an almost infinite number and diversity of activities and projects, ranging from organizing daily activities to planning complex transportation and communication systems that extend around the world and into outer space, incorporating the most advanced scientific, technological, and organizational achievements of Homo sapiens.

In *Planning and Human Survival* (1992), critical problems threatening societal stability were examined. They will not be resolved by natural evolution or fortuitous chance, nor simply disappear for some unknown reason. Without deliberate planning to at least prevent their getting worse, human existence could become increasingly chaotic, with societal catastrophes almost certain to occur, and the eventual disintegration and demise of our species a distinct possibility rather than speculative fiction. The author discussed the failure of the political system in the United States today to provide the type and quality of governmental leadership that is required to guide the nation constructively. He indicated that the mass media of communication are a crucial part of the comprehensive planning required for this directive guidance.

In the United States the mass media have become in fact an element of governance as influential in societal affairs as the legislative, executive, and judicial branches of government. Without cooperation by the mass media, the comprehensive planning by political leaders that is required for complex industrialized societies to function successfully will not be achieved, even if legislators and elected chief executives were supported in their decision making by a fourth branch of government established to provide the information and analysis necessary for effective planning.

In democratic societies, when people conclude that current policies and activities have brought about unacceptable conditions and will produce worse conditions in the future, it is presumed that they will act to obtain the political leadership they believe will produce better societal prospects. When they also realize that organized forethought by the political leadership is required to improve current conditions and future prospects, they will want to know why the comprehensive planning incorporated with increasing success in commercial, industrial, military, and some government operations cannot also be applied in the general public interest to the collective benefit of society as a whole. In time, they will insist that it be applied continually at the critical levels of societal decision making. How can this be accomplished in political democracies? Can it be accomplished in the United States as it is governed today? These crucial questions are addressed in this book.

Since planning is inherent in human affairs, it is necessarily involved in the activities of governments and those public services directed or managed by private enterprise under contract. Some of these activities operate efficiently. Some are conducted by inefficient political bureaucracies to preserve the status quo, with little or no competitive or other constructive motivation. Those that result from "special interests" and "pork barrel" politics usually contribute less to the society than the same human and material resources applied in the general public interest.

At the present time in the United States there is no comprehensive planning by federal, state, and local legislators and other elected officials. They do not evaluate their legislative decisions with reference to the general societal welfare and act accordingly. Politically powerful special interests dominate governmental actions.

Sound planning at the top levels of governmental decision making does not exist. There is no analytical simulation of the society which indicates commitments already made, provides a basis for coordinating existing and projected activities, and evaluates the desirability and consequences of the many different policies, projects, plans, and proposals that are presented continually for consideration, decision, and action.

This critical failure of governmental decision and operational management can be rectified by introducing a planning process that determines the financial and operational feasibility of proposed policies and programs, reveals duplication or conflict among existing activities, and identifies opportunities that can be realized.

Decisions made at the highest levels of federal, state, and local governments vitally affect those living within the political jurisdiction and those outside it affected by the actions taken. But it is these most crucial societal determinations that are the least planned. They take place in a political marketplace for individual self-interests, organized group interests, and partisan political parties. Critical decisions arrived at in this way cannot successfully direct large and complex communities, which require a high order of thoughtful, well-organized planning to allocate available resources among competing needs in the best interest of the society as a whole.

Must we await social disintegration and autocratic leadership to bring about for its undemocratic purposes the comprehensive planning required at the topmost level of decision making for modern societies to function successfully? Can democratic leadership be induced to establish this planning? Can it be effected without abandoning democratic objectives, principles, and procedures?

The author was introduced to different kinds of planning by federal departments and agencies as a young member of the support staff at the U.S. National Resources Planning Board in the Executive Office of President Franklin D. Roosevelt. This early concern with governmental planning was enhanced by his subsequent association as a professor of planning with Rexford G. Tugwell in the graduate Program of Education and Research in Planning at the University of Chicago.

A professor of both economics and political science, Dr. Tugwell learned about the problems of governance and the importance of planning by a succession of unique experiences prior to his directing the Chicago program. These included his role as one of a small group of advisors in the White House during the first term of President Roosevelt when the country was in a severe economic depression, Undersecretary of Agriculture, Director of the U.S. Resettlement Administration, chairman of the New York City Planning Commission, and Governor of the Commonwealth of Puerto Rico. Beginning over fifty years ago he considered the institutionalization of planning in government in many published articles and unpublished working papers and memoranda. The most important of these are incorporated in the selected bibliography at the end of this book.

For his part the author obtained direct experience in business and government planning during seven years as Corporate Associate for Planning (West Coast) at Thompson Ramo-Wooldridge—a large automotive, electronic, and aerospace company—and nine years as a member of the Board of Planning Commissioners of the City of Los Angeles. During a half-century studying various aspects and applications of planning, he has published books and professional papers relating to comprehensive planning and decision making noted in the selected bibliography.

The author considered *Planning and Human Survival* published in 1992 the final book in his progressive examination of the planning process. That is until he was admonished by his wife: "You have described the serious problems confronting the United States. You have written about many aspects and applications of planning, its importance as a determinant of the human condition and our survival as a species. You have told us what is wrong. But you have not indicated what can and should be done."

To determine what should be done, we must not only consider planning as it is practiced today, but how it will be affected in the future by the technological, socioeconomic, and political developments that are changing the nature and functioning of our society. We must also determine how the comprehensive planning required can be conducted in accordance with democratic principles and institutions.

The material in this book relates specifically to the United States, but most of the observations and conclusions apply to other nations as well. If the critical features of effective comprehensive planning are maintained, planning can serve its purpose in modified form in democratic societies with different governmental structures, economic systems, cultures, or societal motivation.

Whether or not one agrees with the particular thoughts and conclusions expressed in this book, the reader will recognize the necessity of some form of institutional mechanism to support comprehensive planning at the topmost levels of governmental decision making.

1

The Existing Situation

> Planning, like any other idea, involves an assumption; . . . that the American public or publics, national and local, will by and large and in the course of time be capable of intelligence in the development of their territories and be capable of the moral willingness to use that intelligence. Planlessness is either or both a lack of intelligence or the moral willingness to be intelligent. The use of the planning approach, planning techniques, the development of planning principles and planning knowledge are consequently a test of the capacity of our people to be a social organism capable of converting its strength and activities into works of social utility and social welfare.
>
> Alfred Bettman, *Planning and National Recovery* (Philadelphia: Wm. E. Fell, 1933)

HUMAN CONSIDERATIONS IN PLANNING

There is an aphorism quoted by planners to support their purpose and their product: "Everyone plans." And indeed this is so. In our daily lives at home, in our work and in our play, we arrange our activities in some way: when and what we do, and in what order. Much less would be accomplished if we proceeded in a random fashion or relied on happenstance, rather than intuition and deliberate design. We plan intuitively or with automatic forethought, without being always aware that we are directing our actions in a predetermined way.

Since we evolved as humans several hundred thousand years ago, we have been planning continuously so that we can survive and prosper. As primitive people we sought shelter from an often hostile environment, slowly learned to forage and hunt for food, and clothe ourselves as protection against inclement weather. Our evolution throughout the millennia has been marked by a succession of achievements in planning: the use of fire for various purposes after its accidental discovery, cultivation of crops, fabrication of many products, collective organization, and the storage and utilization of knowledge for different purposes. Without such progressive individual and collective advancement, civilization as we know it today would not exist.

Conscious planning probably came about accidentally. Controlling fire may have originated from observing fires created by lightning, and learning to light a fire by noting how abrasion can produce heat, smoke, and flame. Learning how to cultivate crops probably originated by observing how nature produces plants from seed. Nature has been the evolutionary progenitor of planning during the billions of years preceding the evolution of humans, in the form of chemical and biological agents directing the development of animate life from a single cellular beginning. By a process of chemical reaction and biological selection animate life evolved. As animals consciously aware of ourselves as mortal individuals and of the environment within which we live, we have existed for an infinitesimal instant in the time it took to create our animal antecedents ranging in size from minuscule amoebas to giant dinosaurs.

Our brief existence during evolutionary time is an important factor in conscious planning. The genetic and instinctive forces which produced us as we are today influence our reactions and actions as much or more than the reasoning we associate with civilization. Underneath the veneer of rational thought and behavior, which we have acquired during the past several hundred thousand years, is a body of instinctual reactions and emotional drives which powerfully affect our emotional reactions and deliberate behavior. As a single example: "The person bothered by noise is more likely to oversimplify social relations or to act impulsively. . . . Many people show increased aggressiveness and annoyance when exposed to noise."[1]

Fear has been an essential instinct for our survival and progressive development. Without it, the natural forces or hostile actions of man or beast which threatened the survival of our earliest ancestors could never have been avoided. Aggressiveness was necessary to meet external challenges with the positive response required to advance progressively, rather than continually retreat regressively. These alternatives are embodied in the term "fight or flight", used to explain the choices we make instinctively before we determine consciously what action we will take when confronted with situations that require immediate decisive reaction. Our strong sense of territoriality is rooted in fear. Animals identify and often mark against encroachment the area required for their sustenance and survival. Primitive people protected the territory critical for them, expanded by modern man to larger and geographically distant economic and political domains. Territoriality is also represented by organizational and hierarchical jurisdictions unrelated to a geographical area. Hate is rooted in our instinctive fear of other people as a real or imagined threat to survival or the status quo, as an object for aggressiveness, or a scapegoat for one's own thwarted desires often fueled by envy or acquisitiveness.

Belief in the supernatural arose from our early reaction as hominoids to awesome events in nature which threatened our existence and survival: violent storms, hurricanes, tornadoes, earthquakes, volcanic eruptions, avalanches, and massive landslides. To propitiate the forces or "gods" that caused such events and thereby reduce the likelihood of their occurrence and psychological impact, superstitions and religious beliefs and rites emerged.

Survival for all animals requires a genetic or instinctive drive to procreate. Male sexual aggressiveness and female receptivity affect our attitudes and behavior more generally. They not only underlie our relations with our sexual partners, but they affect the organization and behavior of family units and many social groups. Sexual preferences and behavior relate to religious beliefs, public health, population demographics, criminality, educational and employment opportunities, and most other aspects of life.

Our fundamental characteristics as social animals give rise to common behavioral traits. The innate fears which favored our survival in primitive times underlie our tendency to react negatively to any proposal or action that "takes us by surprise" and is, therefore, suspect if not threatening. We tend to resist change because we have become accustomed to existing conditions, and change poses the possibility of unwanted consequences. The known present is less threatening than the unknown future. Our preference for the emotional comfort of certainty accounts for our ascribing an accuracy to numbers because they are carried to several decimal places or statements because they are exact, even when, in fact, the precision they imply could not have been achieved in the way they were derived. In the Delphi method of inquiry to obtain the collective opinion of a group of experts, individual responses are required in writing to avoid a strongly voiced opinion expressed repeatedly with self-proclaimed certainty from unduly influencing the judgment and response of others.

Our reluctance to recognize realities is in part because they often run counter to the optimistic wishes and fantasies which support our urge to survive, to live a long time and achieve spiritual immortality. We prefer the pleasure of wishful thinking to the mental and emotional discomfort or active concern engendered if we focus on unpleasant personal or social realities. As discussed later in this book, most people's reluctance to face and deal with realities is a key consideration in planning. They would just as soon ignore disturbing facts, and certainly they do not want to be aware of and worried about them continually.

The prospects of survival for the immediate and extended family are better than for the lone individual. Psychologically, man is both a "lonely island" in his unique and very personal self and a social animal in need of collective human interaction and support. This dichotomy produces negative as well as positive results. The greater security and social satisfaction of belonging to a group of people sharing common beliefs and activities is counterbalanced by the ethnic, tribal, and religious animosities which often emerge. We enjoy the shared certainty of consensus among a group of which we are part. At the same time, we are reticent to join collegial associations because we are innately concerned how other members will act, particularly if they are different from us in race, customs, religious beliefs, and economic and educational status. Our instinct toward socialization underlies our reluctance to hold out as a minority of one against the majority opinion of fellow members of smaller groups such as committees or juries. Under certain circumstances we can abandon the "thin veneer" of civilized collective behavior and act in a way we would not normally consider by joining the emotional outbreak of a mob of looters or some other group engaged in cruel, violent, or illegal behavior, justifying our actions because "everyone is doing it."

Such innate human characteristics are important because planning is by and for people. What can and cannot be achieved and how a plan can be implemented depend on the reactions and actions of those involved. The soundest analytical reasoning is of no avail if it runs counter to human attitudes and behavior that are characteristic of individuals or of groups who propose plans, those who formulate them, and the much larger number of people who are affected by them.

We need only to look about us to observe the ingrained attitudes and spontaneous actions which in themselves present major difficulties for rational planning. Ethnic, tribal, religious, and other affiliations are characteristic of human affairs. Those groups which will not tolerate and actively oppose those who feel, think, and act differently under the law, threaten democratic institutions. In 1993, religious animosities accounted for conflicts around the world between Moslems and those of other faiths, between Sunnite and Shiite Moslems in several countries, between Catholics and Protestants in Northern Ireland, Sikhs and Hindus in India, Tamils and Sinhalese in Sri Lanka. Other conflicts are founded in ethnic and tribal antagonisms and loyalties, often involving territorial claims: the break-up of what was once Yugoslavia, the homelands established or claimed in South Africa, the Tutsi and Hutu tribes in Burundi and Rwanda, the Dinka and Nuer in Sudan. Other civil strife is political and economic in nature with militant minorities battling for control: Communist insurrectionists in the Philippines, the Basques in Spain, Kurds in Iraq, Armenians in Turkey, Tuaregs in Mali. Throughout human history, such divisive antagonisms rooted in the emotional nature of the human animal fuel never-ending wars, civil disturbances, violence, and cruelty.

According to the Carter Center for Peace in early 1993 there were 112 civil conflicts in progress around the world. Thirty of these were categorized as major wars with more than 1,000 battlefield casualties, and ten times as many associated civilian casualties.[2] According to one observer,

> Man—Western man, at any rate, is a cracked vessel: . . . his psychic makeup is the scene for the interplay of contradictions between the primitive nature of his innate impulses and the more refined demands of civilized life, contradictions that destroy the unity and integrity of his undertakings, confuse his efforts, place limits on his possibilities for achievement, and often cause one part of his personality to be the enemy of another. . . . sometimes reaching extraordinary heights of individual achievement but never fully able to overcome, individually or collectively, the fissures between his own physical and spiritual natures.[3]

Human activities always reflect a combination of emotional and rational behavior which varies among individuals, societies, and situations. This dichotomy engenders attitudes and reactions that affect the reasoning and action of those who prepare plans, and of those who are asked to accept them and carry them out. Planners must take these effects on human behavior into account at different stages of the process. Otherwise, they may not understand why people react and act as they do. Failure to identify emotional factors involved will likely create problems in formulating and implementing plans, or cause their rejection. Learning more about the intuitive, emotional component of the human psyche is the province of psychiatry and behavioral psychology. Understanding its operational significance is essential for sound and successful planning.

PLANNING IN PRACTICE

Individuals

Although planning among primitive people was limited because their struggle with nature presented few alternatives, it was crucial to survival. If they did not obtain enough food by foraging or hunting, if they did not cover and shelter themselves to withstand the weather, death was the result and extinction the consequence.

At first, such acts of self-preservation were instinctive. As time passed and experience was consciously recalled by a developing brain, acts of survival and operational advancement were increasingly deliberate. Foraging was fitted to the seasons and to those places where for other reasons food was most likely to be found. Hunting was arranged with regard to the presence, activities, and particular behavior of the prey. Slowly but surely, primitive agriculture and organized hunts developed. How slowly this occurred is shown by the fact that our ancestors learned how to arrange and tend farm plots less than ten thousand years ago, after several hundred thousand years of evolution as thinking animals.

Modern man differs from his earliest ancestors in certain ways and exists in a very different environment. His conscious mind has expanded to include abstract concepts such as mortality, sin, righteousness, guilt, ambition, and a range of personal objectives. Codes of behavior and deportment have come about to control instinctive reactions that are individually or collectively destructive, and to guide our development as social animals toward a more civilized and enlightened community. Systems of law, monetary exchange, administrative organization, collection of data and maintenance of written records, and other societal and religious activities—created in very recent evolutionary times—comprise networks of behavioral interaction affecting our lives in many ways.

In recent times there has been added to the world in which we live an impressive array of new material objects and systems. Beginning with the steam engine, we have developed sources of power for the industrial age: electric generators and motors, engines fueled by gasoline, diesel oil, ethanol, alcohol, and, most recently, nuclear energy. Nuclear explosion provides awesome power for earth excavation in peacetime as well as vast destruction in war. Instruments of communication have multiplied within less than a hundred years to include the telegraph, phonograph, telephone, radio, television, electronic computer, and microwave and facsimile transmission. Transportation has evolved over a much longer time to include animals, sleds, chariots and wagons, boats and ships, bicycles and motorcycles, railroads, automobiles, aircraft, and space vehicles. The telescope and compound microscope, invented less than four hundred years ago, were the first in the long list of scientific instruments now available: electron spectrometer, electroencephalograph, cardiograph, electron microscope, cardiovascular viewers, magnetic resource and laser imagers, and computer assisted tomography. Photography has vastly extended most scientific fields, communications, and our view of the world. The transistor has revolutionized the design and manufacture of modern artifacts of many kinds, and ushered in miniaturization unimaginable not long ago. On the destructive side, weapons of war and military defense have multiplied in number with ever greater accuracy and destructive power. Mustard gas developed in time for use in the First World War, less than a century ago, is now joined by neurological and chemical substances which can kill multitudes of people or exterminate an entire population.

There is no need to exemplify further the remarkable advances in knowledge, which continue at a rapid rate. Entirely new mathematics have been developed. Physics, chemistry, and biology have been vastly expanded in a moment of evolutionary time. The world is a different place than it was only a few centuries ago, and there is every indication it will be as different in the foreseeable future.

As a consequence, the number of "things" to be considered has in itself enormously complicated modern life in the United States: shopping and other tasks required in everyday life; necessary communications; the use and reliable functioning of an increasing number of mechanical devices and technical systems on which we depend; financial, legal, and other operational affairs. Although most of these matters that must be attended to regularly today are less critical for survival than in primitive times, there are many more of them and they require more planning individually and in the aggregate. Some are consciously deliberate: making sure that payments for the home mortgage, utility services, the family automobile, or insurance are made in time. Others are so usual and automatic they are not labeled as such: arranging a day's shopping, which route to take to reach our destination, or properly loading the clothes- or dishwasher for effective operation.

The increasing complication of human affairs brought about by the rapid rate of scientific and technical development requires more and more thoughtful planning by individuals in order to successfully conduct their lives. And as social systems composed of interdependent organizations multiply, human life in general becomes more complex requiring more operational planning by the organizations involved and individuals associated with them.

Groups and Organizations

The human characteristics affecting planning by individuals apply also to groups of people. They may be small or large, ranging from a neighborhood Kaffee Klatsch to associations with thousands of members. They may function informally like a local bridge or garden club, or operate as a formal association authorized or legalized by a larger organization. Some are of only casual interest to their members, others the object of intense and meaningful commitment. They may have a brief life or exist for hundreds of years, concerned only with their internal affairs or actively motivated to affect others. Groups may be politically inconsequential or very powerful. They represent the best and the worst in society, the gamut of good and evil, the sacred and the profane, the moral and immoral, the societally constructive and destructive.

The importance of the hundreds of thousands of small groups in the United States—probably the largest number per capita in any country in the world—is evidenced by the fact that they exist at all levels and in all segments of our society. They are of whatever nature meets the needs or desires of those who have reason to congregate. They express separately and constitute collectively the mix of myriad interests, concerns, convictions, beliefs, and pleasures that are expressed in a democratic society. They represent the purposes of their membership within the society. Some are a means of exerting whatever political, socioeconomic, religious, or other influence each possesses.

As would be expected, group activities involve more than the aggregate of individual planning by their members. To organize, administer, and maintain over time a number of people requires a more structured and formal level of planning. It must take into account the additional complications of collective organization and the many interactions among those in the group.

Private Enterprise

In Austria, all major economic functions are performed by government. In Canada, Japan, and Australia, they are divided between government and private enterprise. In the United States, private enterprise plays a more important role than in any other country in the world.

Production of electricity, gas, petroleum products, coal, automobiles, aircraft, steel, ships, and other major elements of the economy is performed almost entirely by private enterprise. Communication—the most vital socioeconomic function—is conducted by private enterprise, as is most transportation by rail and airway. In every nation except the United States, mail service and railroads are government monopolies, justified by the claim that these most widely used means of communication and transportation are most secure and certain when they are operated by the government. The U.S. Postal Service has yielded most of package mail to private carriers. And in an increasing number of municipalities in the United States, private contractors are performing public services previously provided by government agencies. Governments regulate, set minimum standards, and otherwise affect these activities of private enterprise in the public interest.

Private enterprise in the United States designs, produces, markets, and distributes an almost endless list of products, projects, and services. Those that have been discovered, invented, and developed during the past 100 years constitute an astounding human achievement within this instant of evolutionary time. New means of transportation and new sources of power have been created during this period. Communications have expanded and new materials have been produced. Incandescent lights, clothes and dishwashing machines, electric and gas stoves, microwave ovens, and air-conditioning are recent arrivals in the household.

In applied science and medicine, developments since the end of the past century include new scientific instruments such as the cathode and x-ray tubes, electron microscope, mass spectrometer, gyrocompass and autogiro, wind tunnel, cyclotron, Geiger counter, atomic clock, and of course the electronic computer which is affecting the world in so many ways. Echocardiograph, computer assisted tomography, and magnetic resonance images are among the latest and most complex in a long line of medical instruments produced during the extraordinary time period we are reviewing. Medicines which have been developed include insulin; cortisone; adrenaline; anesthetics; many antibiotics beginning with penicillin; and vaccines for measles, polio, typhus, and different strains of influenza.

The theoretical and basic knowledge underlying these discoveries and developments have advanced in concert: relativity, quantum dynamics, the chemical and structural composition of matter, mathematical and statistical determination, psychological understanding, cognitive theory, and artificial intelligence. Most recently, fundamental knowledge in biology has progressed dramatically since the discovery of DNA, and gives every indication of continuing its rapid expansion.

No military weapon as it existed a century ago compares with its counterpart today. The destructive fire power of the hand gun, the rifle, and cannon is much greater than their predecessors. New mechanisms of death have been produced: the armored tank, aircraft carrier, nuclear-powered submarine, ballistic missile, multiple-targeted nuclear warhead, "smart" weapons, nerve gas, and weapons systems combining different destructive components into instruments of mass annihilation.

This outpouring of discovery, invention, and product development cannot be attributed to private enterprise alone. Universities are the primary source of theoretical discoveries and advances in basic knowledge. Governments have contributed by supporting research and development by military contractors, and by creative achievements in some of their operations. Witness the scientific and technological accomplishments of the Russians—including putting the first human into orbit in space—during the period when all activities in the USSR were operated by a Communist government and private enterprise did not exist.

Personal initiative and creative group effort can express themselves in many ways and in different organizational situations. There is no one political, institutional, or cultural environment required for creative motivation and innovative productive achievement. In the United States, the productive role of business and other private enterprise in the national economy has provided the primary instigation for our remarkable record of creative accomplishment.

These advances could not have occurred without planning. While a creative idea may have been by chance the result of unconscious mental coincidence between an observation and a reactive thought, or the consequence of inspiration and analysis in the preconscious human mind, further refinement and development required planning consciously or intuitively applied. It is impossible to imagine how an airplane, a scientific instrument, a medicine, telephone, or new substance could have been developed from an initial concept to a usable product without deliberate and usually extensive planning.

The combination of private initiative and public concern has been the root of our productive success, now recognized and emulated by other nations as never before. The best balance between these forces—the "checks and balances" in our political structure—is cause for continuous debate, political interaction, and adjustment as conditions, needs, and objectives change. Together, government and private enterprise direct the nation.

Planning is particularly crucial for private enterprise. Unprofitable operations in the business world can continue only until the depressed financial condition forces remedial change, the business is abandoned, or declares bankruptcy. Whatever planning and action are required to restore profitability must be effectuated if the business is to survive. This critical or emergency planning is over and above the operational planning required to arrange financing, product design, production, marketing, sales, distribution, and public and governmental relations. Except in wartime or other national crisis, there is no comparable necessity in government which forces an intensification of planning for organizational survival. The word planning is a descriptive noun appended to more and more executive titles in American companies to describe the primary responsibilities of the position. "Corporate planning" is identified as a staff activity at the top level of executive management in the organization charts of many companies. In the worst business situation, a published "plan" of action to recover is required to emerge from bankruptcy.

Profitability as the driving force in business planning has been weakened during the past several decades by the inability of stockholders to effectively challenge poor performance by executive management. During this period many large companies have operated as executive fiefdoms, with escalating salaries, bonuses, stock options, pension provisions, and other perquisites despite declining profits. This has been especially notable when compared with the compensation executives receive in Japanese companies with superior performance records. It has been said that any executive at the top level of a large American company who has not "feathered his nest" to ensure an affluent retirement has not taken this advantage of his managerial position. Recently, pension and mutual funds and other owners of a significant percentage of the outstanding shares of stock are confronting the executive management of poorly performing companies and forcing or shaming them to make changes beneficial for the enterprise itself and the shareholders who are its owners. Usually this involves more perceptive, intensive, or continuous planning than previously practiced. As both business and the society within which it operates become more complex, poor business planning, management ineptitude, and executive self-indulgence undermine the economic function of private enterprise in a democratic society.

Like most human motivations, the profit motive—the stem of private enterprise and the principal feature of the capitalist system—has its good and bad sides. It provides the initiative which is critical to success: displayed in strong ambition, willingness to take risks, energy, hard work, and optimism. Unrestricted, it can lead to fraud, corruption, monopoly, or complete disregard of the private weal or the public interest. *The Wall Street Journal* reports an increasing number of illegal, immoral, and self-serving acts disregarding all other considerations. Some of these have national and international effects, for example, the savings and loan association scandals of the early 1990s, the political corruption and financial fraud engaged in around the world by the Bank of Commerce and Credit International (BCCI), or the present state of global oil tanker traffic:

> Aging, poorly run ships, ill-trained crews, and poor navigation are giving the world's tanker industry a bad name. . . . Twenty percent of the world's tankers are considered unsafe, yet they continue to operate in vast and busy global sea lanes that remain largely unpoliced. Cutthroat market conditions, shady operators and scant international regulation add to the strain on a system that moves two billion tons of oil and petroleum products annually.[4]

Planning is probably more intensive for illegal and unscrupulous enterprises than it is for legitimate businesses. Laws must be deliberately circumvented, loopholes found and investigated, indefensible activities hidden or disguised, miscreant conspirators recruited, specious excuses and justifications conceived, and escape routes devised if the perpetrators are about to be apprehended.

The bulk of private enterprise in the United States is in small businesses with fewer than fifty employees. Naturally, planning by these businesses is informal, with much less reference data and analysis than is feasible for larger organizations. It may be conducted entirely within the head of the manager or owner. Some form of planning must take place sooner or later or the small business will likely deteriorate. Experience indicates that many small enterprises fail because they do not investigate beforehand the minimum requirements for success. Lending institutions which have funded and subsequently foreclosed small businesses know why many of them fail within a few years. Information obtained during foreclosure may reveal that the proprietors did not have sufficient capital to survive emergency situations, temporary setbacks, or cash flow requirements.

> Undercapitalization . . . is a problem that derails countless small businesses every year, even when their products sell briskly and everything else seems to go well. . . . According to the Small Business Administration, 24% of all new businesses fail within two years and 63% fail within six years.[5]

Or the market they intended to serve could not support the business because population demographics do not support its product or there are too many successful competitors. Or suppliers on whom they must depend for materials or services have proven unreliable in the past. Inquiry concerning the experience of lending institutions with the kind of small business the entrepreneur has in mind may result in abandoning the project or in carefully planning to avoid the mistakes of others.

Contrary to what one might expect at first thought, planning in both business and government is in general weakest at the top level of management. At lower levels there are fewer components to be considered, fewer variables and elements that are difficult or impossible to quantify precisely, and a background of consistent experience to rely on. Lower level planning directly concerned with manufacturing or service operations is normally more immediate, actual, and often simpler than the planning conducted at higher levels of management several steps removed from production. The less complicated the operation, the longer it is likely to have functioned successfully without need for significant change. As a single example, the planning required by each member of a team in order for it to perform effectively is less than that required by the person directing the operations of the entire team. Lower level planning is important, however, because it is an essential part of the entire process and the success of an organization or activity may at times depend on the performance of one of its smallest units.

Planning for the business organization as a whole, generally referred to as corporate planning, involves the largest number of different elements, ranging from those that are operational or financial and can be measured accurately to those that are political or public relational in nature and cannot be quantified. Some decisions may be specific, such as fixing the rate of production, some indefinite, such as establishing a policy which no one knows how it may be implemented in the future, or even whether it can be fully realized. Demands on the time of chief executives are many and various. In addition to the heavy load of duties that accompany the position, exceptional situations require their personal and often undivided attention, such as the possible defection of a customer accounting for a significant percentage of sales, cancellation of necessary insurance coverage, a lowered financial credit rating, potential scandal, or product recall. Any of these could severely damage the public image of the company, maintained at great advertising expense.

> The functions of the executive can be grouped into two categories. . . . One requires the executive to "get up and go" or otherwise act quickly; the other calls for him to "sit down and think" constructively, so he can formulate or approve a solution to a difficult problem, a fundamental policy or strategy, or a longer range plan for the business. One is extravertive and more immediate in its emphasis, the other introvertive and longer range.[6]

The personal characteristics of successful executives can make the second of these functions difficult to achieve. Chief executives attain their positions by ambitious drive and energy, aggressiveness, a willingness to take risks and to make tough decisions. They tend to act quickly and decisively, rather than slowly and cautiously as required at times. Although often thorough and perceptive analysis is not their primary capability, it is becoming essential as business becomes more complicated operationally, more complex technologically, and international in nature. Chief executives do not have the time to personally produce the information and analysis they need for critical decision making.

> To assist [them] . . . . staff planning has come into being to maintain an integrated statistical picture or other conceptualization of the complex of different corporate activities projected into various stages of the future so as to achieve designated objectives.[7]

If this descriptive and prescriptive material is maintained in a corporate planning center, it can be reviewed by those participating in the planning process and those affected by the situation and the plans displayed. They may participate in its formulation. There appears to be no record of companies that maintain a corporate planning staff and center. Some chief executives still assert that they can manage "by the seat of their pants" and conduct all the planning needed within their heads, but the complexities of modern business are gradually dispelling this belief.

Corporate management should be superior in quality as well as authority, for "the buck stops here" with the final managerial responsibility for all activities of the business, separately and together. While top management cannot directly oversee all that transpires within the organization, it must bear final responsibility for what takes place. An organization without final authority is so ineffectual that this situation is unlikely to exist except as a deliberate or inadvertent avoidance of responsibility. Corporate planning helps chief executives to keep in touch to the extent possible with what is going on within the company, since it monitors as well as projects the activities of the enterprise.

A continual difficulty in business and all other planning is our instinctive resistance to change, one of the human characteristics noted at the beginning of this book. Unless we actively want something different, we find the status quo comfortable. We are accustomed to the current situation. Change introduces new circumstances requiring the extra effort of readjustment.

We are skeptical, if not fearful, of the indefinite or unknown future. We prefer the actuality and relative certainty of the present.

The underlying reasons for change, for improvement and the best way to effect it, are revealed and displayed in the information and analysis maintained in the corporate planning centers. In various forms they make it easier for decision makers to identify necessary changes and determine how best to effectuate them, and for those affected by the changes to recognize the need for them and accept the programs developed to carry them out.

Individual and collective reluctance to change underlies the tendency of many organizations to become oversized, in the business world as well as in government. Some managers reason that their reputation, remuneration, and their stature in other people's eyes depends in large part on the number of people they supervise. Naturally they promote an increase in their personnel. Bureaucracies tend to enlarge when the optimism resulting from past success prevents recognition of current problems, and the effects of changing conditions are discounted or ignored until excessive size can no longer be tolerated. Witness the giant losses and employment cutbacks of General Motors, IBM, and other prestigious corporations in the early 1990s. AT&T escaped similar shrinkage because it was already reduced in size by federal antitrust action. Corporate planning soundly conducted reduces the chance of serious mismanagement occurring, unless what it reveals is discounted, emotionally unacceptable, or ignored by those in charge of the business.

> [American Airline's] 1980s "growth plan"—calling for more planes, more routes, more hubs and more flights, and emulated by most of the industry—has been abandoned. . . . In [its] place is the strategy . . . called the "transition plan", it outlines AMR's readiness—indeed, its intention—to change course. Such a change is rare at U.S. corporations, and especially at an industry-leading company where executives' reputations and careers have long been made simply by doing the same thing better than anyone else.[8]

Planning will be even more vital to business success in the future. As the components of the society in which private enterprise operates increase in number and become more technically complicated, the overall functioning of private enterprises becomes more complex. It takes longer for management to comprehend developments, to absorb the rapid accumulation of relevant information, to produce new products or services, to perform necessary analysis, and to prepare and effectuate plans.

As discussed in the next chapter, the world of big business which corporate planning must take into account has changed drastically during the past several decades and will change much more in the future. Advanced systems of immediate communication and fast transportation have spread business transactions, interests, and concerns beyond national boundaries. Production of some goods and services is carried out most successfully far away. Such decentralization brings with it the added complication of adjusting to different labor forces, different native languages, customs, laws, currencies, and monetary exchange rates, often different geographical and climatic conditions. Many companies whose activities were once confined to the United States, now find that an increasing share of their business and their profits are derived from operations abroad.

At the same time, fundamental changes brought about by continued scientific and technological advances must be considered by corporate management: greater use of computers, robots with enhanced capabilities, surrogate intelligence, instant communication within the business and with an expanding number of people near and far. The breadth and depth of knowledge required to perform tasks successfully increases accordingly. In addition, international financial investments and foreign ownership of business enterprises create political issues as well as economic ties interlocking nations in ways that did not exist fifty years ago.

Like corporate planning, small businesses will be affected by developments calling for more extensive use of computers to automatically control machines, for accounting and payroll purposes, to maintain close contact with customers, clients, markets, suppliers, and sources of information. Recent developments that must be followed by small businesses relate to quality control, employee motivation, productivity and creativity, group discussion and decentralized decision making, and other aspects of individual and collective behavior that can affect profitability in an increasingly competitive world.

Two recent developments have added to the necessary scope of planning by private enterprise in the United States: public concern with the effects of human activities on the natural environment, and a change in concepts concerning what is justified in the general public interest. In retrospect it is difficult to understand how unconcerned people were with the physical environment not long ago. It was not emphasized academically or professionally, and reports on the subject by the mass media were few and far between. Only recently has it been brought repeatedly to public attention. Today, it is a foremost political and socioeconomic consideration.

Private enterprise cannot disregard, as it once could, its effects on the surrounding environment. Providing employment, energizing the economy, and paying taxes are not enough by themselves to justify any operational activity regardless of its adverse impacts on the environment. Effects beyond the immediate surroundings are included among those to be considered; for example, those that affect the quality and quantity of the underground watertable, regional air quality and waste disposal sites, or endangered species of animals or plants.

Restrictions on business operations imposed in the public interest have accumulated through the years. Regulations concerning child labor and working hours were among the first, followed by a long list of requirements concerning working conditions, sick leave, retirement, minimum wage, contributions to social security and disability insurance, equal opportunity, and others. Environmentally harmful industrial effluents and waste disposal are no longer tolerated to the extent they once were. Removal of unreasonable requirements or restrictions means appeal to the courts, which is often prolonged and costly.

Conforming to environmental and general interest regulations has increased the operating cost of many businesses. These added costs are passed on to the consumer or customer by raising prices. This may decrease sales volume and profits, in some cases threatening the survival of the enterprise. It reduces the business taxes paid which support the general economy. Since private enterprise is the primary productive force in the American economy, a balance is struck between the operational requirements for a successful business, preserving the environment, and serving the societal interest.

In recent years, the differences between the interests of private enterprise and the concerns of government have been fought out on the political battlefield. Adversarial confrontation rarely results in optimum resolution of these differences. And their far-reaching effects on the condition and prospects of the society are too significant to be resolved by political conflict. A partnership between private enterprise and government must be established to jointly reach conclusions concerning rules and requirements, thoroughly understood and accepted without animosity by both parties. Otherwise, the positive potential of the society is not attained, its stability may be threatened by the reduced efficiency of business and higher prices, and its survival put at risk. Achieving entrepreneurial-governmental harmony will require disclosure of the information needed to determine alternatives, a well-planned procedure of constructive discussion, a cooperative attitude on the part of those concerned, and a full measure of good will all around.

Wrongdoing is as much part of business as it is of most human activities. Examples of corruption, fraud, conflict of interest, false and malicious advertising, and other illegal or unethical acts are reported regularly in *The Wall Street Journal* and other news media. Laws and government regulations are only partly successful in restricting malfeasance within realistic and tolerable limits.

As discussed at greater length later in this book, recent economic and legislative developments have increased the political power of private enterprise. With tax policies and various regulations favoring the availability and use of corporate funds for political causes and campaign contributions, businesses have an increasing advantage in achieving their economic aims by influencing legislation and obtaining regulatory relief.

The globalization of business enables companies to obtain preferential treatment by claiming that otherwise they must transfer operations to a foreign land where occupational or environmental standards are lower or subsidies or regulatory treatment are more favorable than in the United States. Businesses electing to produce abroad reduce employment and otherwise adversely affect the economy of the home country.

> The politics of the global economy, more profoundly than any other issue, puts the self-interest of the governing elites in conflict with the common ambitions of the governed. . . .
>
> What is emerging for now is a power system that more nearly resembles a kind of global feudalism—a system in which the private economic enterprises function like rival dukes and barons, warring for territories across the world and oblivious to local interests, since none of the local centers are strong enough to govern them.[9]

These global developments in the nature and scope of private enterprise present problems of national sovereignty, governmental action in the public interest, and democratic representation for the populace at large never before encountered. In effect, large corporations can now determine the regulations and obtain the legislation that are most favorable to them. Legislation and regulations relating to business are the product of long and determined persuasion by special business interests which have achieved increasing political power through persistent lobbying, campaign contributions, and other elective support.

In the areas of chief concern to business, government in the United States has become the politically symbolic agent for effecting the desires of private enterprise. Since this relatively recent development alters the political scene, it affects planning by government and by business. The change in the balance of public and private interests is as yet largely unrecognized by the public, and the political implications not yet acknowledged or addressed by government or by business. It affects the purposes, specific objectives, and operational tactics of planning by the organizations and individuals involved.

Civil Government

Civil governments plan in two ways. They must conduct enough planning through the established elective, legislative, and regulatory mechanisms to enable government to perform as the primary representative body and directive force in the society. As discussed in the next section of this book, legislatures do not now plan anywhere near enough to fulfill their representative responsibility, exercise enlightened political leadership, or manage public affairs effectively and efficiently.

Governments also plan and administer operational activities, ranging from those needed for national defense to providing public services in local communities. The magnitude of these activities by federal, state, and local governments in the United States is indicated by the amount of money they expended in 1990: two trillion, two hundred and eighteen billion, seven hundred and ninety-three million dollars. Eighteen million, three hundred and sixty-nine employees were involved.[10]

The extent of civil government operations is shown by the activities of the Defense Department. Except for expenditures for Social Security, it plans and manages the largest portion of the federal budget: supporting millions of people, thousands of ships and aircraft, hundreds of thousands of combat and support vehicles, dozens of integrated weapons systems, and services and supplies for the four military services and the Coast Guard operating as a civilian agency in peacetime. The Defense Department also subcontracts and supervises the expenditure of a substantial part of its budget for the manufacture and modification of weapons, support systems, and military equipment by private enterprise.

In peacetime the U.S. Corps of Engineers plans and controls human activities on all the navigable waterways throughout the nation. Over the years, as one of its activities, it has spent billions of dollars on projects relating to flood control, navigation, and operations on the Mississippi River, its major tributaries, and drainage basin occupying one-third of the continental United States. Except for a few toll roads, civil governments plan and operate the vast network of highways constructed under contract by private enterprise. The Postal Service employs 800,000 people, more than any other civil organization in the United States, reaching every corner of the country. State governments operate systems providing police and national guard protection, judicial review, tax collection, and higher education. And municipalities operate police, fire protection, sanitation, and other public services, except when one or more of these are conducted by private enterprise under contract.

Operational planning procedures of government are substantially the same as those of private enterprise, unless they are altered and usually made less efficient by purely political intervention. This may include "padding the payroll" with more people than are needed, in order to acknowledge or create political favors and thereby obtain favorable votes at election time. Sometimes, to attain the political benefit derived from a larger work force, additional people are employed although spending the same money for computing or other equipment instead of for salaries would improve operations far more. Civil service rules established to protect government employees from direct political pressures or demands, as now formulated and enforced, produce such a restrictive categorization of employees and consequent managerial inflexibility that efficient operations are often impossible.

There are other features of government employment which reduce its efficiency compared with private enterprise: a reluctance to establish criteria of acceptable performance, to reward superior productivity and penalize poor production, to terminate employment for cause, provide close supervision, maintain thorough records on the performance of every individual, adopt service fees to reduce political funding and cost-benefit analysis to control size.

There is no substantive reason why planning and managing of government activities should be less efficient than for private enterprises. Both involve people without intrinsic differences other than those usually associated with different personalities, education, particular experience, and those nurtured in the home or work place. These differences apply equally in government and private enterprise. Some government operations are personally appealing because they are interesting in themselves, involve contact with the general public or a particular group of people, or are attractive for some other reason. Increasingly, superior performance and professional achievement in government operations are rewarded in some meaningful way, indicating progress along a clearly defined path of managerial and professional advancement.

Although government salaries in the United States are coming closer to those in private enterprise for comparable work, government employment does not offer the very high salaries, bonuses, stock options, generous pension provisions, and other benefits and perquisites obtained by some executives in business. For some people it provides the personal satisfaction of working directly or indirectly in the public interest rather than for private profit. Affirmative action is practiced more persistently by government than by private enterprise, probably more for political than altruistic purposes. For those with political ambitions and capabilities, some government employment offers public exposure with the possibility of ultimately running for political office. For most of the many million people employed by civil governments in the United States, it is simply another means of making a living.

The particular pressures of some positions in government, such as those directly engaged in law enforcement, are greater than for most employment in private enterprise. But corporate executives in the United States operate under the constant pressure of maintaining short-term profitability and outperforming rival executives within the company and rival corporations competing for a larger share of the market. And for many people working on commission in business, the pressures of maintaining their income can be intense. In general, the personal pressures in government employment are less than those in business, mainly because monetary profit is not the "bottom line" measurement of acceptable performance. In excessively bureaucratic organizations employment can be a sinecure with minimal worries concerning performance or permanence. These exist in business as well as government. In politically promoted positions, security lasts as long as those who made the appointment are in power or until retirement or death if it is a lifetime appointment.

The number and size of government departments, bureaus, agencies, commissions, and bodies increase faster than is justified by population growth or necessary new services. With few exceptions, this is the result of padding the payroll to provide jobs for constituents and other favored people and at the same time a larger block of political support. Public protests have little effect unless they develop into political mandates. Legislators can reduce oversize bureaucracies any time they are willing to reduce the funds they allocate for their operation. They disregard the situation because they do not want to acknowledge their responsibility by remedial action, or they want to preserve the political benefits they may derive from bloated bureaucracies. Campaign claims regularly made by candidates for elective office that he or she will reduce oversize bureaucracies are almost always specious commitments.

Under our present political system, it is next to impossible to reduce oversize bureaucracies, much less to eliminate government entities that are no longer justified for other than purely political purposes. Legislatures do not accept and act on their responsibility and power to allocate funds wisely. And there is no other organization that can monitor the need for governmental action, or the necessary or desirable size, composition, structure, and methods of operation of desirable governmental activities. As noted in a previous section, business develops its bureaucracies, but usually forces inherent in private enterprise correct excesses before they destroy the business.

Business and government planning do not differ significantly in their respective techniques of planning. They employ comparable methods of evaluating needs, formulating objectives, and developing plans. Significant differences arise when purely political pressures make it difficult or impossible for government to function as efficiently as private enterprise. Business creates its oversize bureaucracies, but normally they are the result of mismanagement rather than political interference. The fundamental and supremely important difference between public and private planning is government's unique responsibility of societal representation and leadership, which shapes its general conduct of operations but not its specific technique of planning. The reasons for its failure in the United States are discussed in a subsequent section.

Military Services

There are nations in which the military services are legally or in fact the government. Although they are under civilian control in the United States, they function differently from the rest of civil government in several important respects. They comprise the largest category of employment involving in 1990 1,263,000 military personnel and 911,000 civilian employees. The federal budgetary outlay for national defense in 1992 was $307 billion: approximately $1200 for each man, woman, and child in the nation.[11]

Whereas civil governmental objectives are often unstated or indefinite, and subject to change in their urgency and relative importance, the basic missions of the military services are fixed and firmly stated: national defense, protection of vital national interests, action against hostile threats, and military operations in time of war. The recent humanitarian activities of the military services in Somalia and Bosnia suggest that this may become an additional mission. The best way to attain these purposes may be the subject of debate by Congress, concerned citizens, and special interests—and among the military services themselves. An example of the latter is the decision during World War II by the high command in the United States to defeat Germany in the European theater of operations before committing more military resources against Japan in the Pacific. Some debates are long drawn-out, contentious, and costly, such as determining the feasibility of developing a weapon to intercept and destroy incoming intercontinental ballistic missiles. "Ten years and nearly $30 billion after President Ronald Reagan declared his vision of a shield against nuclear attack, the Strategic Defense Initiative, or "Star Wars" program, is officially dead."[12] Disagreements concerning the nature and conduct of military operations, however, do not alter basic military missions. One of the briefest and most all-encompassing specific missions was the directive to General Dwight Eisenhower as the Supreme Allied Commander for OVERLORD, the invasion of Europe by allied forces during World War II: "You will enter the continent of Europe and, in conjunction with other Allied Nations, undertake operations aimed at the heart of Germany and the destruction of her armed forces."[13]

Planning objectives in the military services are defined in the same way as they should be in civil applications of the process.

> Statements of intention that have been identified, analyzed, and programmed with sufficient specificity to indicate how they can be accomplished with the resources available and within the time limit established. Planning objectives are therefore dependent variables because their specification and selection depend on whether they can be realized. By definition, they cannot be selected as a presumptive preference without reference to their feasibility.[14]

Examples of military objectives from World War II could have been capture and maintain military use of the Remagen Bridge over the Rhine (Army); establish and maintain complete air control over the beachhead OVERLORD (Air Force); locate and sink the battle cruiser *Tirpitz* (Navy); and conquer and control all activities on the island of Tarawa (Marines).

Budgetary provisions or limitations imposed by Congress on activities, projects, or proposed programs of the military services may require changes in specific plans but not in basic purposes. Internal differences among the military and adjustments within the Defense Department to congressional intervention are resolved by the time a decision must be made. Military plans are not drawn out or left unresolved as often occurs in civil governmental affairs. They are, therefore, more detailed and precise than their civilian counterparts. As a group they are the most comprehensive, specific, quantitative, and thoroughly prepared plans in the United States today. In part, this is because they do not involve as many indeterminate elements as do many business plans and most civil governmental plans.

Military planners must occasionally plan "backwards", most often in developing tactical plans. For example, planning an airborne operation involving the transportation of troops commences with the exact time when they must be "on the ground". Everything is planned "in reverse" from this specific deadline: when aircraft must take off to be over the drop area on time, when they must be loaded and ready to go with personnel, equipment, and supplies aboard, when the different elements of this cargo must be requisitioned and collected at the place of departure. Similar operations occur in the civilian sector, for example, a structure that must be built by a certain time or a political campaign that must be completed before the date for the election. Most business and civil governmental planning is directed toward an approximate time for completion, rather than a specific date and even an exact hour and minute in some military operations.

Planning for both strategic and tactical purposes is going on all the time in the military services. It is being conducted by personnel who have had line or operating experience, and are assigned to staff positions to acquire experience in preparing plans or to update their knowledge with the latest developments. They are military officers first, planners second, with either direct experience or a keen awareness of actual operations. This means that plans are realistically related to their implementation in the field, which is often not the case in planning proposed by legislators.

In time of war, threat of war, or grave concern that national defense is inadequate, the military services can plan and complete mammoth projects involving hundreds of thousands of people, a host of organizations, and billions of dollars. The scope of the Manhattan Project to develop the atomic bomb has been widely reported in the mass media, periodicals, and books. Development of the U.S. ballistic missile system in three years in the mid-1950s, capable of delivering multiple-targeted nuclear warheads thousands of miles away, is less well known.

> [It] entailed the expenditure of a billion dollars a year, or three million dollars a day. . . . 18,000 scientists and other technical experts in universities and in industry. . . . Directly and actively participating in the program—from front office to factory floor—were another 70,000 people in 22 industries, represented by 17 prime contractors, and 200,000 suppliers. The project also drew upon a substantial slice of talent in military administration—about 500 officers chosen for technical expertise.[15]

Military planning comprises a hierarchy of coordinated plans: from tactical plans for the smallest unit, the platoon, to successive operational plans for the company, brigade, division, corps, army, and combined forces. Such consistency among the plans of the different components of a military activity is rarely achieved in civil governmental planning. Local, state, and federal governments each find it impossible to synthesize the plans of their respective units, since there is at present neither the political motivation nor managerial capability to achieve such consistency. And coordination between the departments, independent agencies, and legislatures of local, state, and federal governments has presented problems since the early days of the nation: the consequence of state's rights as defined in the Constitution, jurisdictional disputes, regional characteristics and differences, and federal policies concerning state and local governmental responsibilities.

Officers and enlisted personnel in the military services must obey the orders of superiors in the chain-of-command. The protracted procedures of achieving consensus or the lowest common denominator of agreement, characteristic of civil planning, are not involved. However, since people are the most important element in both cases, willing concurrence rather than reluctant obedience is a crucial concern in military planning. With realistic personnel policies, military planning is more readily undertaken and more easily implemented without question than civil planning. There are policies and plans of the military that should be publicly discussed at length in peacetime, but not for the years of argument, controversy, delay, compromise, or postponement often necessary in matters of only moderate significance in civil governmental planning. Problems of primary import are not allowed to continue unresolved until action is forced eventually by crisis. Military plans are debated within the military establishment, often most intensively by those who are primarily concerned with how a plan will affect their military service, its allocation of available funds, or a particular operational preference or personal self-interest. In the future, when the four military services are completely integrated, turf battles will less often obstruct, unduly delay, or force frequent revision of plans for the combined services. In peacetime, military plans are also subject to congressional pressure and budgetary changes or restraints.

Except when they are engaged in wartime operations carrying out prior planning, the armed services are occupied almost completely with various forms of preparatory planning. They must formulate strategic plans for probable and possible military situations or threats, indicating the general or overall form of the military response if or when it is required. Tactical plans are devised for the detailed disposition and maneuver of troops, vehicles, aircraft, and vessels in battle. Plans are drawn for the recruitment of personnel and their training by classroom study, simulation devices, operational exercises, or full-scale mock warfare. Logistical plans are developed for the outfitting, feeding, housing, and other requirements to sustain personnel in their living quarters and in the field. Equipment and vehicles of all sorts must be designed, manufactured, maintained, and replaced. The list of activities and objects that must be planned and procured is almost endless.

At the same time, strategic policy plans are prepared which represent crucial decisions concerning the basic nature and composition of the military forces as a single multipartite entity twenty or more years in the future. They must be drawn within budgetary limits forecast for this future time. With weapons systems becoming more and more technologically complex, requiring highly trained operating and maintenance personnel, the "lead-times" for their conception, design, development, test, and official acceptance is ten to fifteen years. During this period, modifications and revisions must be made as new or improved technology and components for the system become available.

Strategic policy planning starts with the identification and prioritization of potential "threats" to the United States and its vital interests. Part of this projection involves assumptions concerning the probable actions of our allies as well as those of potential enemies or antagonists. A threat of intercontinental or regional nuclear war is very different in driving policy planning than responding to terrorists or guerrillas, or providing humanitarian aid to third world countries. Shall the military forces be large in number with a multitude of standardized and less costly weapons, or small in size, highly mobile, with fewer but the most destructive weapons that can be devised? To what extent should "smart" weapons—self-directed by surrogate intelligence and minimizing or eliminating the human component in the weapons system—be relied on in future warfare? Can such systems be produced to function with the required accuracy and reliability under field conditions in battle? What actions must be taken and results attained to achieve the overall strategic capability desired?

Military planning reflects two great advantages over civil governmental planning in the United States. It is allocated more money than any other category in the federal budget except social security. It has, therefore, at hand many times the money for planning that is available to civil governments. The second advantage is that political leaders and the public at large accept the planning by the military as an essential activity, a necessary and desirable expenditure. Everyone expects the military to plan wisely and well. And if they do not, the quality or accuracy of the plans or their outcome may be criticized, but not the legitimacy of planning itself. This is not the case in civil government.

These advantages have resulted in strategic and operational plans characterized by thorough analysis, clear-cut decision, careful formulation, and prompt implementation. Inevitably, there have been failures. A supreme example was the Maginot

Line, a series of interconnected underground fortifications built between the First and Second World Wars by the French along their eastern frontier at enormous cost over a period of many years. Considered impregnable against attack from the east, it was outflanked and rendered useless in a matter of days by the new *blitzkrieg* form of warfare developed by the Germans.

Because the military services work closely with private enterprises to research, develop, and produce the material and weapons which they provide the military under contract, the logistic plans of the military and the operations plans of business and civil government are generally comparable in quality. This symbiotic interrelationship between business and the military services constitutes the "military-industrial complex", considered by former President and former General of the Armies Dwight D. Eisenhower as a powerful combine which could be misused in setting national priorities.

> From the beginning of the Cold War in the early 1950s, defense spending was dominated by the mutually reinforcing interests of the military, which wanted weapons; the defense industry, which wanted the contracts to build them; and members of Congress, who wanted the resulting jobs in their districts.[16]

Some observers believe that this has contributed to military procurement procedures in the Defense Department that are inefficient, unduly favorable to business interests, and tainted with the corruption endemic in human affairs.

Military operations and planning have contributed to civilian activities in many ways. The designation of "staff" officers to support "line" or command officers, which originated in post-Napoleonic times, has been adopted by business and civil government. "Corporate planning" is a staff activity, part of the office of the chief executive in a business. Congressional and state and local legislative staffs, which have mushroomed in number and size in recent years, provide analytical, operational, and planning support for elected senators and representatives and for members of municipal and county councils. When potential commanding officers and promising young executives are being groomed for their careers, they are assigned for a time as staff to commanders and chief executives to gain experience in support and planning so that they will use such assistance effectively when they are in positions of line authority.

The distinction between "strategic" and "tactical" plans originated in the military services. It has been adopted in business with tactical plans renamed "operations" plans, and to a lesser extent by civil governmental departments.

> Grouping people into sections, departments, divisions, groups and corporations in business and into comparable units in government probably was borrowed from military organization into platoons, companies, brigades, divisions, corps and armies. The succession of managerial levels in government and business also reflects the military chain of command and control.[17]

The managerial concepts of "planning, programming, and budgeting", "program review and evaluation", "critical path scheduling", and "concurrent project management" were first introduced in the Defense Department in the early 1960s.

The military services have developed techniques, technologies, and new materials employed subsequently by business and civil government. Early research in computing machines was underwritten by the military to calculate firing tables for artillery. Aerial photography was advanced dramatically during World War II, and later other remote sensing from aircraft and orbiting satellites developed by the U.S. Air Force and other government agencies has been used in mapmaking, weather prediction, geology, agriculture, urban and regional planning, commercial enterprises, and for many other purposes. New materials and products produced for military weapons have peacetime uses. Research in acoustics and the development of sensitive sonic instruments for submarine warfare have civilian applications. And artificial intelligence may have been first employed extensively and successfully in logistic planning by the U.S. Navy in the Pacific theater. These are only several examples of the transfer of knowledge and material developments by the military services to private enterprise and civil government. This will continue with the further development of weaponry and eventual declassification of information currently withheld for national security reasons.

> In the decade following the Second World War, the Department of Defense became the biggest single patron of American science, predominantly in the physical sciences and engineering but important in many of the natural and social sciences as well . . . spending surpassed its wartime peak (already 50 times higher than prewar levels) by the end of the Korean War, then climbing to dizzying heights after Sputnik, reaching $5.5 billion a year by 1960.[18]

> [Internet] was started by the Pentagon in 1969 as a way to link over dedicated phone lines, large computer databases that could be shared by military and government officials and academic researchers.[19]

Military planning has been discussed at some length because most people and many civilian planners are uninformed concerning this application of the process. In civil governmental planning, plans cannot be formulated, prescribed, and implemented as they are in the necessarily undemocratic and disciplined organizational structure of the military services. While the objectives and instrumentalities of military and civilian planning are very different, the *analytical process* involved is basically the same. It is neither autocratic nor democratic in itself. As noted earlier in this section, methods of analysis and some operational procedures developed in military planning have been incorporated in both civil governmental and business planning. Since the military invest much more in the comprehensive planning process than the civilian sector of society in the United States, its contributions to technique will likely continue.

SUCCESSFUL PLANNING

Before discussing the failure of governmental planning at the legislative level in the United States, it is important to note what can be accomplished by government and private enterprise working together. The most impressive example is the worldwide air transportation system. It required a diversity of planning to cover its many components. Project planning persistently applied over the years was essential to the transformation of these components from their initial rudimentary form to the technically advanced products they are today. Comprehensive planning integrated the components into a single unity functioning successfully as a whole.

Only ninety years ago—one long lifetime—Orville and Wilbur Wright made the "first successful flight in a heavier-than-air mechanically propelled airplane." This tiny craft constructed of wood, wire, and cloth has become the giant airliner carrying as many as 600 people or an equivalent load of cargo. The first flight lasting less than one minute on a beach at Kitty Hawk, North Carolina, has evolved into nonstop flights across the Pacific Ocean on one segment of a route system reaching around the world. The planning involved in the development of components and their integration into a unified air transportation system can only be suggested short of a full-length book.

Planned experiments, research, and improved methods of manufacture changed the outer skin of the aircraft from cloth to lightweight aluminum. Wind tunnel tests streamlined the fuselage. Hidden from view between the outer skin of the commercial airliner and the interior cabin walls, and underneath the cabin floor, is a maze of wires, conduits, ducts, connections, and fixtures required to operate the modern airplane with the flight and engine controls, instruments, communication equipment, and special features which have been added over time. To the inexpert eye they seem helter-skelter, but they are in fact carefully planned or the subsystems of which they are a part would not function properly. Primary connections involving piloting the aircraft are separated to reduce the risk of complete loss of control from localized damage.

The configuration of the aircraft wing has been progressively refined to provide optimal aerodynamic lift; "boundary layer conditions" along its surface which reduce turbulence and drag; an internal structure strong and flexible enough to withstand normal stress and endure exceptional shock; and sufficient space within the wing for fuel tanks, retracted landing gear, and hydraulic or electrically powered lines opeating ailerons, trim tabs, wing flaps, air brakes, and de-icers.

Aircraft engines have progressed in less than a century from the diminutive two-cylinder motorcycle engine of the first mechanically propelled airplane, to those with multiple in-line and radial cylinders, to powerful and reliable jet engines with the thrust required for large aircraft. A single component, the turbine blade, exemplifies the planning, research, and development involved in technological advance. Metallurgical research identified the material that can withstand the enormous centrifugal force acting on the blades rotating at supersonic speed within the jet engine. Experiments, tests, and quality control measures in manufacturing were devised to ensure that blades were free of flaws, since a broken blade can tear a jet engine apart in seconds. When the noise from jet engines at full throttle for take-off made nearby neighborhoods unlivable, sonic research and design modifications reduced noise to an extent once considered impossible.

Early aircraft flew with few instruments: gauges measuring engine temperature and speed, an altimeter indicating altitude, and a compass for geographical direction. Today, the cockpit of a commercial airliner is filled in front, on the sides, and overhead with a hundred gauges, switches, knobs, levers, and handles for controls and alarms: some redundant in case one malfunctions. Modern navigation and automatic pilot systems provide exact location within several hundred meters and a rest for the pilots from manual control of the aircraft. The system can be programmed to pilot the plane from take-off to landing at a distant airport without human intervention of any kind. Not only is the selection and general location of instruments in the cockpit carefully planned, "human engineering" is applied to make them easy to read accurately, and their use compatible with the natural movements and instinctive reactions of human pilots.

Until the advent of radio eighty years ago, communication with the ground was by fly-by hand signals or notes dropped from the plane. Nowadays, voice communication by radio with ground control and between aircraft is highly developed. Collision-avoidance radar is being installed in commercial airliners, and telephones are provided for passengers. Years ago, as an essential requirement for operational safety, the English language and a standard terminology for inquiry and response were adopted for air traffic communication and control throughout the world.

There are some 5,500 commercial aircraft in the United States carrying 465 million passengers during the year. On the average, as many as 75,000 people are aloft over the nation during the day, comprising in the aggregate a community of passengers in the air at the same time. With the increase in the number of airplanes and passenger miles flown, hub airports have become small cities with a population of more than 30,000 people: flight personnel, those engaged in the many ground operations, aircraft and airport maintenance and repair, reservations and ticketing, security and customs, personal passenger services, and general administration. Activities range from highly technical air and ground traffic control to daily inspections of runways and taxiways on foot to remove any tiny debris that could be sucked up by jet engines, damaging the turbine blades and requiring immediate repair. With the larger and heavier aircraft, runways had to be lengthened for safe takeoff and landing, and strengthened to support the heavier loads. They have been equipped with automatic approach and landing systems. The control tower directs and monitors every aircraft on the ground, during takeoff and the longer time taken in approach and landing.

Planning new and improved aircraft and components has always involved a set of essential analytical considerations: strength requirements, weight, payload, fuel consumption, production methods, reliability, ease of maintenance, cost, and safety. None of these can be ignored, but one or more of them may not be applicable in the particular planning at hand. They make planning both more difficult and a more crucial part of the process of producing better aircraft and a better air transportation system.

Extension of air transportation throughout the world has required exceptional political, governmental, and institutional achievements as well as scientific and technical advances. It connects 150 nations with different geographical characteristics, histories, language, forms of government, customs, religion, economic and educational systems, and current conditions. Despite these differences, which usually produce a stalemate in situations requiring collective action, the global air transportation system works. A reservation can be made from a telephone anywhere in the world for a seat on a particular flight between any two places or any number of several hundred thousand destinations, with the near certainty that the seat will be available, the flight completed closely on time, and more safely than any other form of passenger travel. National differences have been subordinated to the advantages of participating in the worldwide system. Political self-interest, parochial preference, or societal prejudice are not allowed to confuse, deliberately disrupt, or otherwise prevent constructive collaboration. However, there is continuing competition among nations and airlines concerning airport access, routes, schedules, and ownership: formalized in "a web of more than 1,200 bilateral agreements, including 72 U.S.-negotiated pacts."[20] A national transportation safety board investigates aircraft crashes and accidents, recommending or requiring remedial action.

It is inconceivable that without skillful and extensive planning the many components of the air transportation system could have been created, progressively improved separately, and integrated into a vast network operating successfully around the world. There have been mistakes, missed opportunities, and unnecessary delays, but the record of accomplishment is evident in the operational success of the system.

The same can be said of the intercontinental and international network of instant communication reaching into almost every locality in industrialized countries and to most places in the third world, involving radio, telephone, television, computers, and orbiting satellites. It is a means of keeping up-to-the-minute coverage concerning events anywhere in the world, of transmitting and receiving particular information or instructions, a mechanism for immediate transactions among financial and other markets separated in time and space, and a way of personally communicating with many people and organizations near and far away.

Because they are the product of scientific and technological developments, there is an intrinsic momentum for continuing growth for both the global transportation and communicating systems. Technical advances are incorporated into such systems automatically as operating experience reveals improvements which can be made. Built-in operational dynamics force change. A static condition cannot exist naturally or be imposed for long. Growth is also encouraged by the desire of most organizations and individuals to be a part of collective endeavors which operate to their benefit and advantage. Participation serves the basic human motivation of self-interest or self-satisfaction. The further development of global transportation and communication systems will affect society profoundly, as discussed in the next chapter.

FAILURE AT THE TOP

As originally established in the United States, the intent and practice of government was representative in a sense that does not apply today. As a member of the Continental Congress, later vice president and president of the nation, Thomas Jefferson traveled back and forth between Washington, D.C. and Charlottesville, Virginia. It took him three or four days by carriage or buggy, stopping overnight at hostels along the way, on rural roads that required fording streams at many places. There was significant separation in time and place between his constituency and his political activities in the national capital. People in Charlottesville learned of Jefferson's activities in Washington days after the fact from newspapers, messages by post, and verbal commentary by individuals returning to Virginia from Washington including Jefferson himself who brought back news when he returned as often as he could to his beloved Monticello.

Legislators were expected to represent the particular interests of their constituency, but also to act in their "best interest" or a larger general "public interest" even when it was not in accord with the current desires of the people at home. Except by courier, there were no instant public opinion polls on people's attitudes and views concerning events, projects, policies, intentions, and future possibilities. There was a delay between the communication of information and the formulation of individual and collective judgments, and subsequent political and legislative action. This interval provided time to absorb the information and understand the issues involved, rather than the immediate response so often solicited nowadays. Furthermore, the mental process of reading the newspaper—the main means of communicating information—was one of gradual absorption and comprehension rather than the instantaneous and more emotional reaction triggered by viewing an event or its photographic portrayal. Also, the time, expense, and difficulties of traveling prevented all but a very few people from going to Washington to meet with their elected representatives in person. The system was one of expected leadership and thoughtful response.

Developments in communication and transportation have radically altered the situation that existed in colonial times. Daily newspapers, telephones, radios, televisions, telefaxes, and computers provide instant communication in different forms, separately, or all together with the increased impact of simultaneous presentation. On the one hand, the time required to inaugurate, conduct, and complete sizable projects increases as industrialized societies become technologically more complex. On the other hand, the time available for careful consideration of critical societal issues, for contemplation, or to await clarifying developments decreases. Instant communication updating information day by day or even hour by hour promotes quick reactions and precipitous responses. Fast transportation enables people to travel to Washington or their state capital to deal directly and immediately with their elected representatives. In the United States today, we function politically and societally in one of two extremes in an era of immediate information: rapid reaction and pressured action, or prolonged inaction because political leaders do not want to acknowledge the major problems that face us until a crisis forces some governmental response.

Election to governmental office today requires extensive exposure on television and radio, newspaper coverage, mass mailings, fund-raising events, and other political activities considered worthwhile requiring all together a large sum of money. In the 1992 presidential campaign, well-to-do individuals, corporations, and other organizations gave some $300 million of "soft" money to the two major political parties. This was in addition to the $55 million of "hard" money each party received from the U.S. Treasury for public financing of the presidential campaign: a total of $400 million. Almost three times as much soft money was collected by the two political parties for use in the campaign, as was provided by the general taxpayer for public financing intended to limit the money spent on presidential campaigns. The third undeclared candidate proclaimed publicly that he would spend $100 million or more of his own money on his campaign, since "you [the public] can't afford to." All in all, half a *billion* dollars was committed to the 1992 U.S. presidential campaign.[21]

At a smaller scale, but no less critical for success, incumbent members of Congress must have several million dollars available to campaign for re-election, which they achieve ninety percent of the time. This near-certainty of permanent legislative employment has resulted in term limits enacted in several states and proposed for the federal government. Congressional candidates running for office for the first time must collect several times this amount unless, as occasionally happens, the candidate is so well known for other reasons that additional identification and public exposure are not needed. The same holds true for state legislators and elected officials in large cities. Money has become the crucial requirement and the determinant for election and re-election to political office in the United States.

There are people who contribute to the campaign fund of the candidate they prefer, with no intention of seeking or accepting some form of reward for their contribution. Knowing the cost of election and re-election, these donors consider their contribution as public-spirited support rather than a privately advantageous investment which some businessmen tout to potential donors as "the best investment you'll ever make." The great majority of political campaign contributors—wealthy individuals, corporations, and other organizations and groups—have some gainful or personally satisfying purpose or possibility in mind. They may maintain publicly that this is their way of getting to know the candidate in person, learning how he or she thinks and intends to operate, and ensuring that their communications with the candidate if elected will be personally considered and answered. There are too many examples of close connections between campaign contributions and governmental actions benefiting the contributor for most such occurrences to be purely conciden-tal or justified for entirely different reasons. To hedge their political bets, some individuals and corporations give generously to both political parties. Some have been known to cover all bets by making annual contributions to every member of a legislature, justifying a request for personal attention should the need arise concerning any of the many matters affected by one or more of the lawmakers.

The rewarding payoff for most campaign contributions is not the legislation itself, but in the broadly stated rules, regulations, or operational requirements which are incorporated in many laws. How they are interpreted, defined, and specified precisely affects the profitability or other vital interests of the businesses, industries, or activities involved.

> Symbolic legislation is passed with fanfare, self-congratulation and the knowledge that the fight has just begun. The participants will decide later, elsewhere, what will actually happen.

> In [Washington], the two staples of trade are the myriad claims on the federal treasury and the commercial rights and privileges that only the government can bestow—licenses for television stations or airlines, the use of public assets like land or water or timber. All may produce vast good fortune for the winners and the competition for them draws many eager contestants. It is bargaining over the law itself, however, that provides the richest commerce and has the greatest consequence for democracy.
>
> Washington . . . engages in another realm of continuing politics that the public rarely sees. . . . This is where the supposedly agreed-upon public objectives are regularly subverted, stalled or ignored, where the law is literally diverted to different purposes, where citizens' victories are regularly rendered moot.[22]

The focus on the exact meaning of the general provisions and particular language of legislation is a primary reason for the proliferation of political lobbyists in recent years: those required to register under the Federal Regulation of Lobbying Act, and those whose "principal purpose" is supposedly not lobbying because they have little direct contact with legislators themselves. It is big business involving hundreds of billions of dollars, 3,000 trade association offices in Washington, D.C. and some 80,000 lobbyists of one kind or another—and the number is growing. In addition, there are legislative lobbyists operating at the state and local levels of government. It is no longer just an occupation or profession. It is an industry.

> It is in relatively small changes to larger pieces of legislation, that big money is made or lost. Careful investment in a Washington lobbyist can yield enormous returns in the form of taxes avoided or regulations curbed.
>
> Over time the sheer persuasiveness of corporate lobbyists has had a major impact on government policy, beyond just the lucrative margin of legislation. The fact that lobbyists are everywhere, all the time, has led official Washington to become increasingly sympathetic to the corporate cause. This is true among Democrats as well as Republicans.[23]

Because they must raise money for election campaigns, our representatives in Washington spend a large part of every day and several hours most evenings campaigning directly or indirectly for money and votes. This can take many forms: meeting with potential supporters, receiving constituents individually and in groups, appearing at organizational functions and newsworthy events, official visits, speeches, social engagements, politically opportune travel, and writing or co-authoring books. Legislators have little time left to consider problems and issues that are not directly related to their political future, much less to participate constructively in planning governmental activities. Their staffs are often the analytical and/or investigative power behind the legislator's throne, determining how the legislator is likely to vote. Recognizing this fact, lobbyists often try to persuade the staff rather than the senator or representative directly.

Legislators avoid controversial issues as long as politically possible, postpone action on critical problems, and resist committing themselves to even short-range plans for fear adverse public attitudes might hurt them at election time. Years ago, one of the most experienced state legislators and political pundits noted, "Legislatures are being weakened by politicking legislators, an increase in special interest groups and internal division. . . . Too many legislators pay more attention to the next election than to current legislative affairs."[24] Special interests are taking up more and more legislative time and attention because their campaign contributions are essential to re-election. At the same time, elected representatives are now so closely tied by modern communications to the voters who elect them—by television, radio, telephone, telegraph, telex, facsimile, newspapers, mail, and computers—that there are few who dare to vote their best judgment if this does not conform with the current attitudes and preferences of the electorate, reported continually by public opinion polls, television and radio news broadcasts, in newspapers, or transmitted directly by any one of the various means of communication.

Legislators are becoming middlemen and women who translate the immediate and often transitory opinions and desires of voters into governmental action: a process but several steps removed from our voting on governmental matters displayed on the television screen at home, our votes recorded, tabulated, and displayed electronically in Washington, the state capital, or city hall. The prospect of the political and operational chaos that would be created by such a development in government is frightening to contemplate.

The overrepresentation of special interests and automatic deference to the immediate desires of the electorate threaten representative democracy because it trivializes or eliminates altogether consideration of the community as a whole and its collective best interests, which at times do not coincide with voter preferences of the moment. The welfare of the societal entity is not represented, unless it is assumed to be symbolized by the collection of special interests and voters' current desires. This is not the case, since the special interests that can afford sizable campaign contributions and the considerable cost of successfully lobbying the legislature to their advantage are by definition and motivation not concerned with resolving major problems of society. And often the current desires of the electorate do not take into account what is in the general and longer range best interest of the entire community, or even what is required for it to continue to function. There is usually a time lag between the emergence of critical societal problems and their recognition by the body politic and its willingness to do something about them. The public is reluctant to accept "bad news" in general, and particularly to defer popular preferences because of unpopular problems.

As one example, the electorate does not recognize that there are some 350,000 hazardous bridges and thousands of miles of deteriorated highways in the United States which will cost over $350 billion to replace or repair. And there are over 750 urban areas with populations over 50,000 which will require $100 billion to reconstruct deteriorated water systems, many of them leaking hundreds of thousands of gallons every day. Many more billions must be spent to maintain aging public utility systems in operating condition, and over $100 billion to clean up dangerous waste disposal sites, and to recycle municipal waste and find new places for its disposal. These expenditures must be made if our transportation and urban utility systems are to continue to function, and hazardous waste sites are not to pollute underground aquifers, poison surface runoff, and endanger human health. When money is budgeted for these purposes, it is not available for other uses the public prefers. Public reluctance to "bite the bullet" may delay action until the situation becomes so intolerable that the body politic finally acknowledges that expenditures must be made, and allows its elected representatives to act accordingly without their committing political suicide, at much greater cost, however, because of continued deterioration during the years of postponement.

A similar situation has existed for years with respect to the national debt: $4.3 *trillion* in mid-1993, almost $17,000 for every man, woman, and child in the United States. The public is now alerted to the increasing percentage of the national income that must be spent paying the interest due on the national debt—in mid-1993, fifty-seven cents of every dollar collected by the Internal Revenue Service—which continues to grow as we borrow from ourselves in order to spend more than we receive in revenues. People are generally aware of the adverse effects of this fiscal imbalance on the prospects of future generations that must bear the heavy financial burden it imposes. The more interest they must pay because of money borrowed by people in the past, the less they will have to spend on facilities and services they desire. Our federal, state, and local governments have yet to face this reality and act accordingly. Until recently, legislators have been unwilling to even mention the word "tax" except to deny the necessity of tax increases. They have yet to demonstrate that they will vote for the increases they know must be imposed at some time. Every effort is made to assess "hidden" charges or indirect costs which the body politic will not identify as tax increases. It remains to be seen whether the voting public and its political leadership will take the steps required in the national public interest to resolve this basic societal problem, or whether the nation must await a crisis of almost revolutionary nature to force remedial action.

The failure of elected representatives to act in the general public interest is supported by political organization and operating procedures favoring fragmentation. Almost all legislators represent areal subdivisions of a larger governmental entity: federal congressmen a state; assemblymen geographical areas within the state; and city councilmen electoral districts within the municipality. As ethnic groups increase in number and political awareness, they seek subdivision of the governmental jurisdiction into electoral areas that allow them to vote together as a cohesive block, thereby achieving greater direct representation and political power. The proliferation of special governmental districts providing a single or several public services also increases political fragmentation, adding new operational jurisdictions to the long-established areas constituting the electoral base of regular representative government. And most recently, metropolitan urban areas and other regions—distinct from existing political jurisdictions—are proposed to relate governance more directly to the geographical disposition of natural resources and human activities as they occur in space.

These developments fragment rather than unify decision and action by government in the best interest of the political entity as a whole. Elected officials representing the entire electorate are relatively few: the president of the United States, governors, mayors, and a few city councilmen-at-large. Legislators each representing a part of the whole are legion: 535 in Congress, thousands in state governments, and hundreds of thousands in counties, municipalities, townships, districts, and regions throughout the nation. Inevitably, each legislator focuses on satisfying those who elected him, on reciprocity and tradeoffs with other legislators which strengthen his or her political position and the likelihood of re-election. Unspoken agreement among members of legislatures can ensure that they do not interfere with each others' decisions in their own districts—especially those that involve substantial campaign contributions—even when these harm the political entity as a whole. At the federal level this takes the form of the "hold—the power of any Senator to block a vote on a bill or a nomination for any reason"[25]—a method of forcefully favoring local rather than national interests.

Legislative actions that benefit the governmental unit as a whole are limited to those that do not in any way threaten re-election. Partisan politics are commonly carried to the point that what is good for the political party and its attaining or retaining political power is more important than constructive collaboration in the general public interest. The filibuster, amendments and riders, committee appointments and manipulation, and a hundred and one procedural devices have been designed to further political partisanship. Whichever of the two major political parties in the United States wins an election, the other immediately concentrates on winning the next election rather than cooperating at least for a time on the common good.

In local governments when political parties are not important, other forms of partisanship develop.

The time is long gone when outstanding public-spirited citizens took time off from their regular activities to serve as legislative policy and decision makers in federal, state, and local governments, and representatives of the people back home. This part-time service has become a full-time occupation, providing permanent or long-time employment for incumbents, with many perquisites, privileges, and contacts. Many who retire or are not re-elected accept positions as political advisors or active lobbyists with private enterprises seeking governmental action of some kind—actually not such a reversal of roles considering the attention paid to special interests when they were members of the legislature. In recent years, misconduct by our elected representatives has increased, causing early retirement and voluntary or forced resignation because of corruption, unethical acts, or immoral behavior. Fewer and fewer of the most capable and reliable people in society are willing to run for public office.

As noted at some length later in this book, the modern mass media of communication determine or profoundly affect all aspects of American life. They have become, in fact, the fourth element of government, together with the executive, legislative, and judicial branches established by the Constitution. Public response and reaction are affected by family, friends, casual contacts, experience, education, and other informational and attitudinal inputs, but people in the United States obtain almost all their information concerning current events, the issues and individuals involved, and their relative importance from television, radio, and newspapers. In recent years, issues of national significance have not only been extensively reported by the mass media, but television has become a means of news analysis, public debate among proponents and opponents, and political and ideological presentations to "win friends and influence people." Besides broadcasting public meetings and events on certain cable channels, network news programs are being used increasingly to conduct indirectly governmental and other societal affairs.

On the average, television is viewed over seven hours a day. The radio is turned on frequently in the home and in the car. Newspapers are read or perused by millions of people. Increasingly, the media utilize or report the same material. A story appearing first in a newspaper is abbreviated and recast for presentation on TV or radio, or vice versa. Newsworthy research published in a professional journal is reported in layman's language in the mass media. Reports by a foreign correspondent or the local representative of an international news agency in faraway places, difficult or very expensive to cover, are shared and presented to the public by all the media in their respective ways. As a consequence, the body of information disseminated to the public at large by the different mass media is essentially the same, its effect magnified by consistent and repeated presentation in different forms. If repeated, reaffirmed, or referred to often enough, it determines more than any other informational input the reactions and conclusions of the public concerning the subjects presented, the people and organizations covered, and directly related matters.

As interacting systems are developed linking television sets, telephones, and computers, a wide variety of programs and special services will coalesce on electronic screens as the primary source of information and related activity for most people. Far more than is the case now, these screens will become the informational, analytical, and operational center for most individuals and households, businesses, and governmental bodies. If by chance or by design they present and emphasize a particular subject long enough, they can produce a public reaction and force a particular responsive action which both business and government leaders think are unjustified, a mistake, and not in the general public interest. Criminal activities, fraud, scandal, unethical behavior, or gross mismanagement cannot be concealed nor corrective action ignored when they are reported on hundreds of thousands of telecomputer screens.

Identification and exposure on TV, radio, and in newspapers is essential for election and re-election to public office. And the mass media determine in large part public evaluation of the performance of elected representatives while they are in office, and therefore their chances of re-election. Legislators are ever aware of the public perceptions formed in the minds of their constituency by the mass media, which influence them personally and affect their political careers. They are alert to how they can use or influence the media to their political advantage. Since the mass media never sleep, this is a constant concern, emphasizing immediate effects and actions rather than longer range developments and more thoughtful consideration.

There is not enough time in the calendar day to communicate all the information that exists which is relevant to all the subjects of importance or of current interest at any given time. Which subjects are covered in broadcast time and newspaper space available, and how much information about each of those selected is provided, must be decided before it is presented to the public. This selection of subject matter and its treatment has been going on since the first newspapers and broadcasts. Limits of time and space also prevent treating in depth the subjects selected. The average viewer, listener, or reader can absorb only so much in the limited time or space available. Comprehension of this material is enhanced if it is expressed in simple language understood by most people, or in several languages in multilingual societies where this is necessary for communication which is not discriminatory.

Information and its communication are required for any society to function. In a primitive community, information is transmitted among its members and from generation to generation by word of mouth and by example. In our industrialized society utilizing modern science and technology, information and communication are its vital lifeblood. We are now at the first stage of a revolutionary expansion and advancement in the provision and exchange of information which is described and discussed in the next chapter of this book. Since intensive and widespread use of the most modern communications is relatively recent, it is difficult to determine to what extent they may have contributed to the failure of political leadership. It is clear, however, that they must participate constructively as the fourth element of government if our society is to function effectively and prosper.

"Failure at the top" is doubly disturbing when we take note of the super-serious problems which confront us today. First and foremost is the avoidance of nuclear or biological war somewhere in the world, which could spread progressively among nations armed with the latest weapons systems. Within the United States unemployment leaves millions of people financially and emotionally distressed. It is difficult for the increasing number of people with educational deficiencies to find jobs, and participate constructively in a society steadily becoming more complicated. There is less and less housing that lower income families can afford. Crime, violence, terrorism, and drug and alcohol addiction threaten societal stability. The poor, the destitute, and the homeless constitute an increasing percentage of the population. To these fundamental problems must be added costly operational requirements that must be met if society is to continue functioning, including new or expanded facilities and services for more people; replacing or repairing essential transportation and utility service systems; disposal of waste; permanent storage for highly toxic nuclear waste with a half-life of several hundred years; controlling pollution of the air, surface waters, and underground aquifers; and preserving essential features of our ecological habitat. Since many of these problems are interrelated, their resolution requires collective consideration and action with respect to a few or many of them at the same time. Such a unified approach, the comparative analysis involved, and collective action it requires are very difficult to achieve in our democratic society as it functions today.

There is no overall plan by our civil governments that addresses these problems separately or in concert. They are approached sporadically, with an unwillingness to acknowledge the seriousness of the situation. Rather than coordination of effort, there is persistent disagreement among governmental agencies concerning what should be done, when it should be undertaken, and who should do it. The allocation of available resources is more political than analytically justified. The result is management by crisis. In states allowing initiatives and referendums, voters must resort to these direct means to break legislative gridlock and force governmental action on fundamental problems and longer range objectives the electorate believes are crucial.

It is not that we do not know how to plan comprehensively. The previous sections of this book have referred to impressive planning conducted by individuals, groups and organizations, private enterprise, the military services, and civil governments separately and as joint endeavors. It is at the topmost legislative levels of government—the most important of all—that comprehensive planning is not being applied. Our elected representatives do not even conduct the planning required to carry out their basic responsibilities effectively: collecting revenue, borrowing money, allocating available resources among requirements and needs that are never fully met; enacting laws and formulating regulations; protecting persons and property; providing public utilities and services. How well these basic responsibilities are met determines more than any other activity or event the current condition and the prospects of the governmental jurisdiction involved. Although external developments and unusual events can affect the governmental entity significantly, comprehensive planning will at the very least maximize what can be achieved in a given situation. To completely fulfill their responsibilities, our elected representatives must also decide what to do about critical problems that will take years to resolve, establish longer range objectives, and identify policies in the general public interest to be implemented gradually as opportunities arise.

There is now no organization responsible for evaluating legislative government, promoting its improvement, and overcoming built-in bureaucratic resistances to change. The ultimate and only power today that can effect improvement and change in government is the body politic, which must be sufficiently aroused to take collective action or to apply the necessary political pressure. At present, this is possible only after a near crisis has developed. None of the forces requiring change in private enterprise normally apply to government: declining sales and profits, mounting losses, bankruptcy, antitrust restrictions, competition, strike or boycott, and adverse developments nearby or far away. The federal government and its bureaucracies seem to be immune to fundamental change short of a social revolution. Failure at the top is less severe at the local level, where government is somewhat simpler, where there is more direct contact between elected representatives and their constituency, where some public services may be performed by private enterprise under contract, and public-private cooperation and joint action are more likely. Nonetheless, the problem of bureacratic oversize and destructive inefficiency persist at the local level of government.

> "We're trying to get the policy-makers (legislators) to confront the issues."

> "City government is disjointed and too disorganized. There's no central division, no hand that coordinates the various departments. There has to be a fundamental reform of the existing layers of bureaucracy."[26]

Whether the presidential election in 1992 represented a rare instance of public opinion forcing more effective legislative action concerning major problems of the nation remains to be seen. Increasing the effectiveness of legislative government and improving its functional operations is probably the most difficult task of planning in the United States today.

CAUSES OF THE CONDITION

Various reasons are given by different people for the serious deficiencies of our legislative governments. Population growth is considered by many as a primary cause. Providing new facilities and services for new additions to the population—together with the much larger and more costly task of replacing or repairing the existing infrastructure—requires a very large expenditure of money over many years which is not available for other needs. Some point to the gradual breakdown of the "traditional family unit" and the consequent loss of moral, educational, psychological, and financial support which it provides, together with the devastation of individual lives and the fragmentation of many families caused by rising drug and alcohol addiction. Others believe that the combination of serious problems which confront us today overwhelm the managerial capability of legislative government as it exists today. Some maintain that government undertakes too much; much more could be accomplished if more were left to private enterprise operating through market mechanisms.

The primary cause for our condition is more fundamental in nature and portentous for the future. We inherit basic human characteristics that cause us to react and to act in ways that do not contribute to resolving the awesome problems being created in large part by scientific and technological advances. This simple statement requires careful explanation.

It has taken billions of years for the earliest forms of animate life to develop into human beings as we are today. Our existence as thinking animals is an infinitesimal moment in the billions of years it took for us to develop. Imagine a flexible ruler stretched tight around the 25,000–mile circumference of the earth, representing six billion years of evolutionary development since the earliest forms of animate life appeared. Our emergence as Homo sapiens some 200,000 years ago represents about eight-tenths of a mile on this circular ruler 25,000 miles long. We are an extremely recent addition to animal life on earth.

During the billions of years in which chemical materials and biological protoplasm evolved into human beings, animate organisms developed directive forces that were essential to the creation, survival, and emergence of progressively more resilient forms of animal life. After eons of gradual evolution, these internal directive forces became a bundle of instincts enabling the human animal to avoid danger, to reproduce successfully, to attain greater safety in numbers, and to identify those elements of the environment that support rather than threaten human survival. A sense of territoriality developed, since primitive people were aware of the land area required to provide food, water, and other essentials for survival. Fear of the unknown or that which was distinctly different, reluctance to change from habits established by experience as bearable or beneficial, became part of the package of survival instincts. An innate aggressiveness—a positive rather than a passive or regressive stance—favored individual and societal advance, as did bonds among members of the immediate family, collaboration among the extended family, and cooperation by the entire clan or tribe. But hostility or at least extreme caution was the appropriate response upon meeting strangers, encountering territorial encroachment, or any other potential threat to individual survival or societal well-being. An intuitive doubt, hesitancy, or distrust concerning collaborative action in general reduced the possibility of adverse as well as beneficial consequences.

Instinctive reactions constitute the core of emotional man formed over millions of years. Rational man, aware of his reactions and conscious of his actions, is less than 200,000 years old. Civilization has developed as an evolutionary addition to natural selection to prevent the self-destruction that could result from unconstrained emotional reactions in the world as it exists today. A set of beliefs, customs, rules, requirements, laws, and procedures has been formed to guide human society constructively and hopefully ensure the survival of the human species. Initially passed on from generation to generation by example and word of mouth, civilization was first codified in the form of written history only some 6,000 years ago, about 130 feet on the time-scale of six billion years represented by the 25,000-mile circumference of the earth. Man's effort to consciously control his reactions and direct his actions to enhance his prospects for the future is a recent development, not yet by any means an assured achievement. Despite the emergence of rational man and the beginning of civilization, the behavior of most people is emotionally driven rather than rationally derived, the product of instincts more than careful, contemplative, deliberate thought.

Animate life has had to adjust to great changes in the physical world: cataclysmic volcanic and atmospheric events; radical changes in the land masses, oceans, mountains, and vegetation. Most of the adjustments have been gradual, extending over many millions or at least many thousands of years. In their brief existence, humans have had to adjust to ice ages, climatic changes, and other environmental events. At the beginning of recorded history 6,000 years ago, the size of the human population was less than ten million. It is over five and one-half billion today.

The changes having the most impact on human society have been brought about by the phenomenal development of science and technology during the past several centuries. Beginning with the Industrial Revolution in England 300 years ago, there has been an awesome increase in the breadth and depth of both basic and applied scientific knowledge. Intellectual and professional fields of knowledge have advanced dramatically, including physics, astronomy, chemistry, biology, mathematics, medicine, pharmacology, psychology, and engineering. Entirely new fields have emerged: artificial intelligence, computer science, robotics. As indicated previously in this book, an incredible array of new products of every kind and description have been conceived, designed, manufactured, and distributed far and wide; most of them within the past 100 years. New natural and synthetic materials have been produced and used for new purposes. New systems of transportation, communication, and production—consisting of millions of interrelated parts—have been devised, constructed, and installed nationally and internationally.

As societal systems become technically more complex, they require operators with above-average education and often special training. And unless the systems can be designed to be especially "user friendly", their employment by the ordinary user for more than the simplest purposes calls for more than the average education. Most technically complicated activities require operators with particular skills, but fewer people may be needed as automatic controls and directive devices are incorporated. As more and more scientific systems are established, a larger and more highly educated group of operators—but a smaller percentage of the total population in countries with rising populations—is needed to manage these basic societal functions. There is a widening gap between those with educations that fit the technical needs of today and tomorrow, and those who do not have the requisite education and cannot therefore participate directly. This growing educational gap is in addition to the more widely publicized economic gap between the "haves" and the "have-nots", the wealthy and the poor.

A society can be imagined in the future in which the essential functions must be managed and controlled by a few of its best educational members. The rest of the people act accordingly. This is the case now in part. There are functions in the United States which we use and consider essential, over which we have no control as individuals other than bargaining on some minor aspect or choosing a competitive service if such exists. Insurance, banking, telephone communication, public utility systems, and tax collection are familiar examples. Only if a large number of people act together over a period of time can these systems be changed in any fundamental way by the ordinary citizen.

Science involves objective observation, demonstrable facts, and established interrelationships expressed logically in quantitative, mathematical, or other terms. Its validity is confirmed by reproducing the observed or predicted results. Emotions are involved, but science is the product of structured observations, rational reactions, logical deductions, and consistent actions. Illogical, irrational, or purely emotional responses disrupt or invalidate scientific systems. Since most people react and act emotionally, the systems do not function successfully unless they are insulated against irrationality. If for these reasons most people cannot participate directly in the formulation and operation of systems important in their daily life, they are likely to become discouraged, frustrated, or angry. As more and more societal functions are controlled by computers, robots, and artificial intelligence, the role of the average individual becomes more and more programmed for him. Actions and activities that do not fit operating scientific systems are anachronistic or unproductive.

We are at a transition stage in evolutionary history. Until several hundred thousand years ago, our instincts unconsciously guided our progressive development as individual animals and as a species. As we acquired the capability to think and reason consciously, we have been able to gradually exercise a greater degree of self-direction, beyond that dictated by the instinctual directive forces which have guided animate life successfully for so many million years of evolution. As our mental capacity and store of knowledge expanded and deepened, and we discovered new sources of energy, our power to transcend environmental limitations and direct our development increased, to the point that we can obliterate or poison and render uninhabitable large sections of the earth, deliberately or inadvertently. With the worldwide transportation and communication systems we have produced, human communities can no longer function in isolation. Humanity as a whole is acquiring the power of self-direction and of self-destruction. As time passes, the present differences in these capabilities among countries will diminish and eventually disappear.

Confronted with the inexorable advances of science and technology, humankind is being forced to think and act more realistically and rationally. It has accumulated the basic knowledge and the technical means of achieving continuous societal improvement. At the same time, it has the emotional predilections ingrained over the years which can lead to progressive societal deterioration and partial or even total self-destruction.

Human political and social behavior have not produced favorable conditions for the future. The world today is ravaged by wars which have occurred regularly since the precepts of civilization were introduced to reduce their frequency and eventually eliminate them. Rather than pursue this objective, societies with highly destructive weapons of war sell them to whoever has the money or credit to buy them. The jobs involved in manufacturing military weapons must be preserved whatever the consequences. Undeclared armed conflicts, insurrection, violence, and terrorism are rampant. Drug and alcohol addiction are widespread. Dislike and prejudice exceed compassion and understanding. Corruption is endemic. Tribal, ethnic, religious, cultural, and other differences real or imagined spawn hate, cruelty, injustice, and hostile actions. In many nations, majorities and minorities, the haves and the have-nots are approaching open conflict.

This is indeed a dismal and frightening scenario. Unfortunately, it is also a fact. It is children and adolescents, the largest segment of the world population today, who are most affected by these conditions. Their prospects for the future are dim, and their participation in constructive change the most difficult to achieve. Whether people can change their behavior which has produced the present situation is the most crucial question of our time. Because technical considerations are involved in more and more societal functions, rational reactions and behavior must prevail. Emotions are an essential component of individual and social behavior and accomplishment, but they can be disruptive or destructive when they dominate the political scene. In dictatorial, autocratic, or oligarchic societies, the population must conform to the will of the individual or small group with absolute power. In a democratic society, the situation is very different and much more difficult. In the United States, significant changes in the present reactions and actions of the body politic are required for successful governance. Also required are changes in the present operations and an additional societal role for the mass media of communication; vast improvements in public and private education; and fundamental changes in legislative motivation, procedures, and decision making. The welfare of the nation and society as a whole must be considered above individual and special interests. Mutually constructive collaboration between government and private enterprise is essential.

How such major accomplishments could be attained in a democratic society currently undergoing far-reaching changes brought about by major developments in communication is the subject of the last chapter of this book.

REFERENCES

1. Gerald W. Grumet, M.D., "Sounding Board, Pandemonium in the Modern Hospital," *New England Journal of Medicine*, 11 February 1993, pp. 433, 434.

2. Ex-President Jimmy Carter, Interview, *McNeil Lehrer News Report, Channel 28*, 15 February 1993.

3. George F. Kennan, *Around the Cragged Hill, A Personal and Political Philosophy* (New York: W. W. Norton, 1993), p. 27.

4. Ken Wells, Daniel Machalaba, and Caleb Solomon, "Unsafe Oil Tankers and Ill-Trained Crews Threaten Further Spills," *The Wall Street Journal*, 12 February 1993, p. A1.

5. Brent Bowers, "This Store is a Hit but Somehow Cash Flow is Missing, Undercapitalization is the Commonest Form of Torture for Entrepreneurs," *The Wall Street Journal*, 13 April 1993, p. B2.

6. M. C. Branch, "Logical Analysis and Executive Performance," *Journal of the American Academy of Management*, April 1961, p. 27.

7. Melville C. Branch, Jr., "Psychological Factors in Business Planning," *Journal of the American Institute of Planners*, Summer 1956, p. 177.

8. Bridget O'Brian, "Tired of Airline Losses, AMR Pushes Its Bid to Diversify Business," *The Wall Street Journal*, 18 February 1993, p. A1.

9. William Greider, *Who Will Tell the People: The Betrayal of American Democracy* (New York: Simon & Schuster, 1992), pp. 393, 401.

10. U.S. Bureau of the Census, *Statistical Abstract of the United States, 1992*, 112th Edition (Washington, D.C., 1992), pp. 280, 305.

11. Ibid., pp. 336, 338.

12. "Reagan's Missile Shield in Space, 'Star Wars', Is Pronounced Dead," *The New York Times*, 14 May 1993, p. A10z.

13. George C. Marshall, *The Winning of the War in Europe and the Pacific* (New York: Simon & Schuster, 1945), p. 10.

14. Melville C. Branch, *Planning: Universal Process* (New York: Praeger, 1990), pp. 47, 48.

15. Lt. Col. Kenneth F. Gantz, Editor, *The United States Air Force Report on the Ballistic Missile, Its Technology, Logistics and Strategy* (Garden City: Doubleday, 1958), p. 30.

16. Thomas E. Ricks, "With Cold War Over, The Military-Industrial Complex Is Dissolving," *The Wall Street Journal*, 20 May 1993, p. A1.

17. Melville C. Branch, *Planning and Human Survival* (New York: Praeger, 1992), p. 108.

18. Herbert Mitgang, review of Stuart W. Leslie, *The Cold War and American Science*, The Military-Industrial-Academic Complex at M.I.T. and Stanford, in *The New York Times*, 1 June 1993, p. B2z.

19. Walter S. Mossberg, "Internet, A Vast Link That Isn't Missing, Can Be Hard to Find," *The Wall Street Journal*, 13 May 1993, p. B1.

20. Bruce Ingersoll, "Big U.S. Airlines Fly Into Foreign Barriers Over Expansion Plans," *The Wall Street Journal*, 14 May 1993, p. A1.

21. "The Best Campaign Money Can Buy," *Television, Channel 28.* FRONTLINE. WGBG Educational Foundation and the Center for Investigative Reporting, Inc., 1993.

22. William Greider, *Who Will Tell the People: The Betrayal of American Democracy* (New York: Simon & Schuster, 1992), pp. 124, 106.

23. Jeffrey H. Birnbaum, *The Lobbyist, How Influence Peddlers Get Their Way in Washington* (Times Books, Random House, 1992), p. 4.

24. Jesse Unruh, "State Legislative Weakened, Political Science Students Told," *USC Trojan Family*, 10 July 1979, p. 20.

25. Norman Ornstein, "Senatorial Choke Hold," *The New York Times*, 18 May 1993, p. zA15.

26. William McCarley (Chief Legislative Analyst) and Michael Woo (City Councilman and 1993 Mayoral Candidate) in Karl Schoenberger, "The Urban Jungle," *Los Angeles Times*, 30 May 1993, p. D5.

Intellectual leadership as opposed to catering to mass reaction; the long view as opposed to the short one; the readiness to accept immediate hardship and to take the immediate risks with a view to averting much greater ones in the distant future . . . these things are not for the legislator with another election looming imminently before him; they are not for the official caught up in the vast networks of modern governmental bureaucracies and subservient to the primitive assumptions on which these latter usually operate; they are not for the political leader daily measuring his popularity by the reactions of the television screens and the public opinion polls, harried hourly by a thousand different duties and problems of his office, and beholden in countless ways to the impressive posture and the effective slogan for the success of his effort.

George F. Kennan
Foreword to Norman Cousins,
The Pathology of Power (W. W. Norton, 1987)

2

Critical Areas for Societal Advancement

> Man is a strange animal; he doesn't like to read the handwriting on the wall until his back is up against it.
>
> Adlai E. Stevenson, quoted in James Reston, *Deadline* (New York: Random House, 1991)

As noted in the preceding chapter, planning is an inherent element in all human actions. In its earliest manifestation as a directive chemical and biological force, it has guided the evolution of animate life over billions of years. It functions preconsciously as an intuitive force directing human actions. It has been applied consciously throughout human existence to produce an impressive array of physical projects and to organize individual and social behavior for many purposes.[1] A brief indication of its myriad applications in human affairs today is the primary purpose of chapter 1.

This chapter considers the two areas of human activity that are most crucial for society today and tomorrow: communications and government. All human activities are of course interrelated in one way or another, closely or remotely, to a greater or lesser extent. However, to treat all of them separately and all together with their myriad interactions is intellectually impossible and also unnecessary. There are always certain elements in every activity that are most determinative in general or at a particular time.[2] The two covered in this chapter affect society more than any others because they are basic; society cannot function without communication and some overall controlling element in its political organization. And the most serious problems confronting the United States today and threatening its future involve communications and government. Resolving these problems will not be achieved without deliberate, thoughtful, and effective planning. They are the subject of this chapter. What can be done to solve or mitigate them, and establish a sound basis for societal survival and advancement, is the subject of the next chapter.

COMMUNICATION

Communication has been the essential characteristic of animate life since its beginning. If chemical and biological forces did not interact with changes in the external environment, and instigate corresponding evolutionary changes in the next generation of organisms, animate life could not have evolved to progressively higher levels of development.

> "No man is an island, entire of itself," John Donne wrote [1593–1631]. Surprisingly, the same is now turning out to be true even for bacteria, the simplest of organisms. . . . All bacteria seem to be able to act as groups and communicate with each other.[3]

Such interaction, critical for evolutionary advance, is a form of chemical and/or biological communication. Humans have interacted with their environment in order to survive. We have learned to communicate with each other automatically, without conscious awareness by facial expression, bodily movements, or odor; and consciously by gesture, sign, spoken and written language, and abstractions such as mathematics and the visual arts. Without communication, individuals and societies could not exist, and their advancement is a function of effective communication more than any other factor. Communication makes possible the acquisition and dissemination of knowledge, conceiving and completing projects large and small, family and societal functioning and survival. It is the essence of animate existence and action.

As noted in the previous chapter, scientific and technological advances have revolutionized communication during the past 200 years, after billions of years culminating in the development of spoken and written language and its reproduction by printing. The mass media of communication have become a vastly expanded and impactful force in society during the past 100 years.

Television

Of the mass media, television is affecting most profoundly every aspect of society. In the short span of sixty-six years it has become a global phenomenon. More than one billion TV sets are operating around the world, a 50% increase in the last five years. This number is expected to increase 5% each year, more than twice this rate in Asia where more than one half of the 5.5 billion people on earth reside. "TV sets are more common in Japanese homes than flush toilets. Virtually every Mexican household has a TV, but only half have phones. Thai consumers will buy a TV set before an electric fan or even a refrigerator."[4] In those areas of Brazil where printed materials are scarce and illiteracy is high, television is the main means of communication for its population of 150 million people. It is the principal source of information and entertainment. Almost anywhere in the world a TV antenna can be seen on the roof of a house or hut. In most communities there is a forest of antennas indicating the presence of television communication in many or most homes. Over 98% of households in the United States have an average of two TV sets. More than 53 million of these households have cable television, and about three-quarters have video cassette recording equipment. In Belgium, it is reported that 95% of homes receive at least twenty-five cable channels: in 1993 the highest exposure per capita to this medium of communication in the world.

The number of television channels available to the ordinary viewer and the range of programs and special services provided are increasing. In Europe, the number of channels has more than tripled from 39 to 120 during the past decade, and may reach 250 within three years. In the United States, "The nation's biggest cable television company announced . . . that in early 1994 it would install technology that would ultimately let its customers receive as many as 500 channels."[5] The range of material broadcast and the special services offered free or pay-per-view will expand dramatically, depending on the prospects of advertising revenue or other benefit, the willingness or capability of people to pay for particular programs or services, and public subsidy.

It is also clear that dissemination of the forthcoming abundance of channel choices will be available to an increasing number of television viewers. Satellite dishes are being installed all over the world to receive the growing number of TV channels. Their spread is inevitable as they become smaller, and affordable for more and more people:

> Kuwait City rooftops are a sea of parabolic antennas. Vans roam Bogota streets with miniature satellite dishes on the roof and a megaphone blaring promises of hookups for $150. In New Delhi, "dish wallahs" nail satellite receivers to crowded apartment buildings. Nearly 20% of all Polish households have installed a dish over the last three years. The Ivory Coast distributors have so flooded the dish market that they can no longer give them away.[6]

More than 300 TV services are now delivered by satellite, and the number is increasing rapidly. Global super-channels reach hundreds of millions of households. The major world news broadcast (CNN) is seen in 137 countries, three-quarters of the 191 nations in the world. There are plans to launch scores of additional communication satellites in the next five years.

Private enterprise has provided the main motive force and monetary investment for the explosive growth of television. Advertising revenues have made it possible. Worldwide spending for TV programming was about $65 billion in 1993, growing about 10 percent per year. Approximately one-half of this was in America, half in Europe and Pacific Rim nations. Television programs are a major U.S. export, amounting to about $2.5 billion annually. Within a few years, the costs of just transmitting TV programs globally is expected to exceed $6 billion. About $20 billion a year is spent for military intelligence derived from satellites. In 1990, the three major television networks in the United States paid over $800 million per year to broadcast national football league games. These few figures indicate the enormous sums of money involved in television production, programs, distribution, personalities, and related activities. It is a big stakes business, with large profits to be made by some and substantial losses by others in what is developing as a mammoth worldwide contest to attract large audiences, revenue, and profits. It has been said, "Ownership of TV stations is tantamount to running a money machine that churns out profits in good times and bad."[7]

Computers

At the same time that momentous developments are occurring in television, there has been vast expansion in the use of electronic computers. There were probably sixty million IBM compatible personal computers in the home in 1991, ten million Macintoshes. This does not include the millions used in government, business, universities, and other organizations. Total sales of consumer electronics in the United States grew 4.1 percent in 1990 to $33 billion, and is expected to expand at approximately this rate for years to come. The price of computers with the same capabilities has declined steadily. Their capabilities, however, continue to expand and account for any price increase. Processing power doubles every two years or so, memory more than tenfold every five years. New analytical, display, and programming features are being added continuously. The dramatic spread of computers needs no statistical confirmation. It is to be seen on all sides: in more and more homes, offices, laboratories, production plants, educational institutions, medical facilities, and as part of almost every human activity.

Computers are being interconnected into networks that provide the benefits derived from intercommunication among many people and multiple sources of information, located anywhere in the world where there is a microwave connection.

> Worldwide, up to four million scientists are thought to be wired into the rapidly expanding maze of intercontinental networks, which now number 11,252 and are known as Internet. . . . "It shrinks distance and time to zero. It is as if all the world's scientists were in one room, available at one computer. Needless to say, this is having a profound impact on the way science is done."[8]

In 1991, there were more than 32,000 "bulletin boards" in North America, 45,000 worldwide, providing intercommunication among millions of people using computers for many purposes. Every board on the Fidenet can choose to carry messages on any of about 450 topics. Fidenet extends into more than fifty countries, including such nations as Macaw, Botswana, and Greenland, not usually associated with high technology. Hundreds or thousands of personal computers are being interconnected in parallel for a different purpose: to provide in concert enormous computing powers equaling or exceeding those of most supercomputers at a fraction of the cost.

Interactive Services

Computers and television sets come together when "interactive services" are made available. Computers are needed to produce and present the proposed services, many of which are or will be displayed on television screens in the household, office, laboratory, and other locations. "Many computer scientists and telecommunication experts believe . . . national and even global computer networks will fiercely compete—or even replace—traditional television and radio networks that broadcast over the air or transmit by cable."[9]

At the present time there are far more television sets in households throughout the world to receive the increasing number of TV broadcast channels and preferred interactive services, than there are computer screens to receive the same information. Whether household computers will reach the number and wide distribution of TV sets remains to be seen. Computers may be designed and manufactured which display on their screen the range of visual images now available only on television screens. Or television sets will be designed and produced that permit the manipulation of numerical information and visual images now possible only on computers. More likely, the television set will be combined with the computer according to "one of the few media visionaries in the Anglo-American world, a person who understands the growing importance of global television in the modern media framework," who predicts that

> The television set of the future will be, in reality, a telecomputer linked by fiber-optic cable to a global cornucopia of

> programming and nearly infinite libraries of data, education, and entertainment. . . . [It] will revolutionize the way we are educated, the way we work, and the way we relax.[10]

It is not farfetched to project a time when a single screen will display for most people what newspapers, journals, books, radio, libraries, and other repositories of information now provide separately. With computing capabilities incorporated in the receiver, certain material portrayed on the viewing screen can be examined in different ways, manipulated to explore or project particular aspects, and printed out for further use or reference. Less remains to be accomplished technically than in reducing manufacturing costs, providing the disposable income to purchase the set, or distributing it free because of direct savings it brings about or indirect economic or other benefits derived from its use. There is no question of demand. TV sets are the first purchase of choice, rather than necessity, among the poor in countries around the world. Subsidizing their acquisition and use may prove advantageous for government and/or private enterprise. Some municipalities in the United States find it cost-effective to subsidize the installation of low-flush toilets, which do not require the unnecessary gallons used by old-style toilet tanks. As a consequence there is no need to find and develop new sources of water for an increasing population. In time, government and private enterprise may find it worth while to subsidize in like manner an interactive television-computer in every household to provide information and services, and to conduct transactions of many kinds.

The handwriting is on the wall, and the first examples of the communication revolution are at hand. In France, the Minitels network is serving more than six million households in 1993. An impressive diversity of 20,000 services are offered, including, for example, news; sports scores; personal finances, bank account information, check review, transfer of funds; credit card purchases; taxi reservations; fax messages; grocery orders and delivery; used-car prices; wine prices; electronic telephone directories; Michelin guidebooks; legal dictionaries and research; and erotica.[11]

> Iowa is already broadcasting classes on portions of the state-owned network, which will consist of a 2,800-mile web

> of thin glass fibers that will connect all 99 counties when it is finished next fall. . . .
>
> By next October, the network will have tied every county to Iowa's three universities, 15 community colleges and 11 private colleges, the state's eight public television stations, and all state government offices. . . .
>
> The next phase will tie in the state's 351 high schools and more than 500 libraries. And a bill currently before the legislature would authorize extending service to all hospitals both public and private.[12]

What the future will bring in the way of concentrated communication systems providing a long list of sources of information, personal services, and entertainment—and when this might occur—remains to be seen. How many of the population will choose, be able, or can afford to use them? In 1993, the school system of the Los Angeles Board of Education enrolled 640,000 students: 87% ethnic minorities, 65% living below the poverty line, and 40% unable to speak English. It is difficult to imagine how such a population can be educated without fundamental changes in our current system of education, which will include widespread and intensive use of interactive computers and television. More generally, in the most optimistic scenario,

> Wireless communications, intelligent software and miniaturized machines are expected to come together in a futuristic world of easy-to-use hand-held "personal digital assistants". In theory, these machines will respond to written or spoken commands, communicate with other people's hand-held computers, and retrieve and display everything from movies to scientific documents.[13]

Impact

It is generally recognized from personal observation and published facts and figures that television has proliferated and spread to the far corners of the world. This means of visual and aural communication is an essential element in almost every household in economically and technologically developed countries, and will in time be extended to every community in the world and probably to every household. Those concerned with communication and its societal impact agree that the mass media will become increasingly crucial in the lives of individuals and society at large: as television and radio broadcasts, computer programs, newspapers and other information services, popular magazines and professional journals, movies and videotapes, and the contents of libraries and other repositories of information become available on one or more consoles in the home and eventually on portable instruments carried by hand.

Precisely what form this vastly expanded communication will take, and how long it will take for it to be effected, cannot be predicted at this early stage in its development. Private enterprise seeks to establish interactive systems of television and computer communication which serve millions of people continually, with the implicit or stated objective of substantial profits, prestige, and political influence. The U.S. Federal Communications Commission establishes technical specifications for broadcasting stations, ownership limitations, restrictions on advertising time, prohibition of indecent content, "equal time" for opposing political polemics, and minimum time for children's programs. There is no overall statement of basic policy covering all societally significant aspects of the mass communication systems.

The separate efforts of individual and corporate entrepreneurs in communication businesses are directed by their respective situations, special interests, and particular objectives. Implicit in these competitive activities is the assumption that they will produce—individually and collectively, without any general directive policy and few operational constraints—a desirable if not optimal outcome for society as a whole.

> Companies, betting on the emergence of a vast digital industry, are jockeying for position in what they expect to be its three distinct segments:
> —the *content* of digital transmission, such as databanks, consumer services, music, books, and movies
> —the *delivery* of information over telephone lines, cable TV, satellites or other wireless networks
> —the *manipulation* of information with operating software, personal computers, hand-held communicators, TV control-

lers, and the like, to let consumers filter and customize the flood of data to fit their needs.[14]

There are significant differences of opinion concerning the impact and societal function of television as a mass medium of communication that underlie all discussion on the subject. One group believes it should provide what audience ratings indicate people want. Their desires define what should be shown on television. A few restrictions are justified—such as prohibiting the deliberate instigation of public panic, extreme violence, cannibalism, or intercourse and explicit pornography among humans—although some viewers would accept or even welcome some of this content on the television screen. Such minimum limitations on the freedom of expression guaranteed under the first amendment of the U.S. Constitution are justified, provided they do not reduce audience response and ratings, advertising income, and profits.

In general, the concept maintains that the broadcaster should determine the content and presentation of information on television in accordance with viewer preferences. It assumes that TV reflects but does not create or shape individual and collective attitudes, beliefs, or opinions. Therefore, whatever is shown on television is justified since it reflects some reality of human existence, confirmed by some viewer preference. Those who find the content uninteresting, distasteful, or otherwise objectionable can and will tune into another TV station or turn the set off. This view presumes that television involves no significant societal considerations other than those expressed by viewer preference. Since the inception of television some sixty-five years ago, entertaining its viewers has been the predominant objective and commercial profitability the measure of successful performance.

Experience, observation, and research refute the contention that TV is not deterministic. The selection of what is to be broadcast has important consequences in itself, since it determines what will be seen and what will not be seen. There is always far more material available than can be broadcast in the twenty-four hours in a day and night. If the material selected is also broadcast repeatedly, its impact is increased since a single presentation is usually soon forgotten or attention is diverted to other subjects. If the same material is presented emotionally rather than as a simple fact, its immediate impact is greater and it is remembered longer and more vividly than if it is presented calmly.

All information presented by the mass media is deterministic to the extent it is accepted without question as accurate or truthful by its recipients. If it is not reliable it has misled, created or contributed to mistaken reactions or false attitudes, and perhaps brought about unjustified actions. There are notable examples of deliberately false advertisements on TV, erroneous or exaggerated claims for products, facts and figures broadcast that later turned out to be premature or mistaken. In every such instance, the material presented had produced unfortunate consequences, large or small, important or unimportant as the case may be. Of course, accurate and truthful information is important, if not critical, not only in mass communication but throughout the community in general. Although it is never attained completely, every effort to achieve it is societally desirable: especially by the mass media which are the main source of public information and have such widespread and lasting impact.

Innocent until proven guilty is not presumed when unfounded or mistaken allegations are broadcast on television. False statements are not questioned. The initial presumptions of guilt and accuracy are never erased completely in the minds of the millions of viewers who received and absorbed the mistaken assertion or erroneous information, even when retractions or corrections are publicized. Careers can be destroyed or created overnight, conclusions disseminated that cannot be corrected or erased. Witness the perpetuation and enhancement of the Elvis Presley myth over many years, the popularization of entertainment stars, and the unjustified damage done to people by widely publicized false allegations. False accusations of child abuse, which are later retracted, linger in the minds of some of those who initially heard and believed them. The fact that television can produce such effects and immediate consequences makes it unrealistic and senseless to maintain that the mass media do not impact people profoundly and shape or determine some of their actions.

The normal difficulties of determining accuracy and defining the truth, which apply throughout society, are compounded by technical developments in procuring and editing television images. Photographs can be altered in ways that cannot be detected. "With digital imaging the manipulation of photos is easy."[15] Sound tracks can be doctored to incorporate audible reactions which did not occur: laughter responsive to humorous quips, enthusiastic crowd response at public performances and political events, and applause or no audible reaction by people in various situations. Favorable reaction expressed "loud and clear" can be erased, and replaced with a negative reaction or the "dead silence" of no reaction at all. The sequence of presenting newsworthy events, repetition of dramatic broadcasts, or regular use of unflattering pictures of prominent people affect the impact of the broadcast material. "Even in news programs, deft editing can make a person speak sound bites out of context."[16] "Media ethics are breaking down. We're in a period of manipulation of information."[17] Technical and procedural alterations must, therefore, be considered together with the inherent difficulties of maintaining accuracy and truth.

> A larger and larger proportion of our experience, of what we read and see and hear, has come to consist of "pseudo-events", that is, events that have been staged or concocted by publicity agents, entertainers or spin doctors for public dissemination. Debates are pseudo-events; so are talk shows, press conferences and interviews. Whenever in the public mind a pseudo-event competes for attention with a spontaneous event in the same field, the pseudo-event will tend to dominate. Whatever happens on television will overshadow what happens off television.[18]

Large-scale deception on TV now involves much more than broadcasting the results of massive campaigns of letter-writing, telegrams, telephone calls, faxes, and computer messages to elected officials, organized by special interests, as if these were an expression of the entire body politic. Paid publicists, lobbyists, and political and business advisors are conducting bigger and better deceptions, which even the most suspicious, cynical, and perceptive television viewer, radio listener, or print reader cannot identify as such.

> The era of vox pop . . . has meant boom times for at least one species of Washington insider: consultants who deliver

> populist rage. . . . Unlike old-fashioned letter-writing campaigns . . . the new campaigns are sometimes intended to appear spontaneous. . . . The rise of this industry has made it hard to tell the difference between manufactured public opinion and genuine explosions of popular sentiment.[19]
>
> "I saw the Iraqi soldiers come into the hospital with guns. They took the babies out of the incubators . . . and left the children to die on the cold floor." . . . The incubator story was the centerpiece of a massive public relations campaign . . . for a fee of $11.5 million. After the war, the group revealed that it was financed almost entirely by the Kuwait government. . . . No infants had been dumped from their incubators.[20]

The owner or broadcast supervisor of a television station, or the owner or editor of a newspaper, bears primary responsibility for the accuracy and appropriate presentation of the information they transmit to the public, although they do not produce it themselves and cannot check it. Nonetheless, they are in the best position to require corroboration of information, and to refuse to disseminate material that would have a damaging impact until it is confirmed or disproven. This is becoming more difficult as human knowledge expands and is increasingly specialized. But it remains supremely important for the constructive conduct of society. "A popular government without popular information, or a means of acquiring it, is but a prologue to a farce or a tragedy . . . a people who mean to be their own governors must arm themselves with the power which knowledge gives."[21]

The mass media compete aggressively among themselves for the advertising and other promotional dollars which support their operations and provide substantial profit. Competition among television stations, networks, and cable systems is especially fierce. A reduction in audience ratings quickly reduces profits. This leads to the adoption or development of whatever means or methods will retain and attract viewers: by the owners of television stations and systems, producers, authors and scriptwriters, program directors, camera crews and other operation personnel who authorize, create, select, prepare, or present the substantive material which is broadcast. Inevitably this calls for more and more dramatic and emotional treatment, which appeals to our instincts deeply rooted in millions of years of evolutionary development, rather than the rational element of our personality developed during the very brief period of civilization. Emotional man is responsible for never-ending war and undeclared armed conflict, latent and active tribal and religious animosities, widespread human violence and cruelty. Unrestrained competition in television exploits the emotional, instinctive, and primitive components of our character.

Anyone who has watched TV regularly day and night during the early 1990s, with an analytical eye and ear, will have observed the progressive increase in the depiction of violence on the screen: expressions and acts of cruelty, sex just short of explicit intercourse, more and more gun play, armed conflict, aggressive attacks, and destructive actions. This has occurred in the selection of movies for presentation on television, and in programs written expressly for this medium. The violence is depicted without personal or societal retribution for illegal, cruel, sadistic, or licentious behavior. Even network news programs focus on vivid events rather than the most important newsworthy happenings. Many are mostly crime and police reports, distorting the image and representative activities of the community. This escalation of emotional and aberrant content affects viewers generally. Its impact on children is especially significant since they are tomorrow's leaders of society.

> Accumulated research clearly demonstrates a correlation between viewing violence and aggressive behavior—that is, heavy viewers behave more aggressively than light viewers. Children and adults who watch a large number of aggressive programs also tend to hold attitudes and values that favor the use of aggression to solve conflicts.
>
> The average American child, watching around three hours of television a day, has by the seventh grade witnessed eight thousand murders and more than a hundred thousand other acts of violence.
>
> Of the hundred and eight half-hour shows . . . between October [1992] and February [1993], in only less than 10% of them did the viewer have to survive without at least one story about sex or violence.

In 1991, the Motion Picture Association of America rated only 16% of American movies as fit for kids under thirteen.[22]

This explosion of violent content in TV programs is part of the intense adversarial competition among broadcasters for high audience ratings. "There's an incredible amount of research to support the fact that there's way too much violence in television."[23] "Whether it's China or Czechoslovakia, wherever you go, America is seen as a violent nation. We export this image in our films and television programming."[24] Besides affecting viewers in general, the portrayal of violence is strongly suggestive for viewers engaged in or susceptible to criminal activity.

> Critics of the news media who deplored the broadcast of the murder said it was not the brutality of the scene that made it offensive; it was the lack of a compelling reason to show such brutality. "There are occasions when death and blood are part of the news."[25]
>
> One of the great unresolved issues of television news: whether compelling pictures should be allowed to dictate coverage.[26]
>
> News reports about criminal innovations can quickly produce imitations on a national level.[27]
>
> A Frenchwoman is suing the head of a state-owned television channel for manslaughter after her seventeen-year-old son was killed by a home-made bomb that she said he learned to make from [an] American television series.[28]
>
> At a time when America is struggling with a rising tide of violence, Paladin Press enthusiastically peddles primers in the techniques of violence. Its books are well known to police and federal agents who have found them in the libraries of serial killers and bombers.[29]

In the constant quest to attain or maintain profitable audience ratings, TV reporters and camera crews seek situations with emotional and dramatic content that attracts us intuitively. Rationally, we may welcome or deplore the content, but we can neither ignore it nor immediately dismiss it. To obtain the news story or add another "angle" to an existing one, the TV microphone may be thrust into a person's face and the camera close-focused to catch the shock or pain of someone who has just suffered a tragic loss, a survivor pinned under a collapsed structure, or the victim of a traffic accident waiting for the mechanical "jaws of life" to release him from the wreckage. Video film capturing some unusual or aberrant aspect of the private life of well-known people is sure to enthrall TV viewers. Fascination with and the widespread use of dramatic images with high emotional impact are epitomized by the videotape of the Rodney King beating: shown more often, more widely around the world, and for more different purposes and reasons than any other single event in television history. It has, in fact, been imprinted on the minds of contemporary TV viewers, newspaper and magazine readers, and the human consciousness in general to the fullest extent this can be done. "New research in laboratory animals is beginning to explain why people best recall emotionally charged events."[30]

In its search for exciting news involving every aspect of human behavior, television accepts few limitations on its right or what it considers its obligation to intrude to the extent necessary into private affairs. Reporters objected to their not being allowed to accompany troops into combat during the Gulf War in 1991; military security was considered less important than instant news. When the U.S. Navy Seals landed uncontested on a beach near the airport at Mogadishu, to support famine relief in Somalia, "more than seventy-five reporters and camera crews were waiting at the beach with microphones on and videotape rolling."[31] It might be argued that television would be responsible for an earthly "giant step forward for mankind" if it could cover armed conflict in progress so closely, immediately, and realistically—without editing or censorship—that public revulsion would outlaw war. Unfortunately, no attitudes or actions by people have been successful in mitigating, much less eliminating, this foremost scourge of humanity.

In the United States, probably more than in any other country, advertising is the lifeblood of television and radio, less for newspapers, and least for the telephone system functioning as a public utility. Since this income supports operations and produces the profit, the needs and desires of advertisers determine in large part what is shown on television and broadcast on radio.

The print media also depend on advertising revenues, but they are less subject to direct control of substantive content. An old adage summarizes the interrelationship: "He who pays the piper, calls the tune."

The largest advertising expenditures are for television exposure; over three billion dollars were spent in 1991 on viewers averaging eighteen hours per week world-wide, forty-seven hours per week in the United States. Presumably, such sums would not be spent without some measure of their positive impact on the sale of the products and services advertised. Advertising on television serves many purposes: selling products and services; providing news; promoting public events, particular causes, different religions, political candidates and activities, and public and private beliefs and institutions. It takes many forms, including carefully formulated statements or sales "pitches" broadcast before, during, and/or after regular programs; "infomercials" combining entertainment and unidentified advertising in a single program; incorporation of selected products in the staging or mentioning them in the script of regular programs; announcements of upcoming programs to entice viewers to stay tuned to the TV station; and sale of "blocks" of time to advertisers or promoters to use as they see fit, subject to limitations imposed by the Federal Communications Commission. In recent years, subscriptions to TV channels and "pay-per-view" for special events provide another source of advertising revenue. And there are promotional "packages" combining television broadcasts with the availability of articles decorated with advertising logos or statements—or other "freebies" or purchasable objects—as part of the overall advertising campaign.

Advertising in the United States accepts few limits. It appears on the clothes of professional athletes, in the sky above for the captive audience below, and on the inside surface of the doors to toilet stalls and on toilet paper for the edification of those using these facilities.

> Between 1965 and 1990 the number of commercials shown on network TV tripled. We encounter an estimated 3,000 marketing messages daily. Every day, by one reckoning, more than eighteen million of us get a call from a telemarketer trying to sell us something by telephone.[32]

> Advertiser-produced video news releases . . . are increasingly turning up on television news programs. These "news" stories . . . are shrewdly produced by publicists so that stations can seamlessly air them as though they were genuine news, rather than the advertising they are.[33]
>
> There's real concern that infomercials are being used to push bogus products. There is more than the usual share of fraudulent advertising through those infomercials.[34]
>
> Block programming dates to the beginning of radio, and it is estimated that hundreds of the country's 10,000 stations currently sell significant amounts of time.[35]

While the substantive content of television is determined in large part by commercial advertisers who foot the bill, political advertising on television has more profound and universal effects. Few observers dispute the fact that exposure in the mass media of communication is essential for election and re-election to political office in the United States. Otherwise, voters must choose among the names on the ballot, with only the information obtained by word-of-mouth, hand-distributed political pamphlets, or personal appearances by candidates at public places. Since television is the main medium of mass communication today and the primary source of news for most Americans—and the combination of TV and personal computer destined to become an even more pervasive and persuasive cornucopia of information in the future—its impact is most crucial in the arena of political choice. The large campaign funds required today for election and re-election to political office are spent mainly for the necessary television time. The political advertisers paying for exposure are those with special interests including business corporations, wealthy individuals, professional bodies, political parties and action groups, large unions, supporters among the electorate, and just about anyone with a vested interest to be realized and the money to pay for television time.

Political success is next to impossible without television. The power of the medium to trigger emotional reactions and shape public attitudes and conclusions is confirmed by continuous market research directed to this end. "Sound bites", brief statements carefully formulated to arouse emotional reactions and engender public attitudes and political choice, are perhaps the best known of the media methods developed to "make friends and influence people." They are as likely to be exaggerated, misleading, or false as they are to be accurate and true. Mass communication has been subject to misinformation and manipulation since its inception not so long ago. As the range and intensity of this most crucial element of society increase exponentially with rapid technological development, its significance for society increases correspondingly. As a single indication, "CNN (Cable News Network) reaches two hundred countries and more than 16% of the world's eight hundred million TV homes."[36] Political leadership is attained and retained in technologically developed countries through television "advertising", and legislative actions in democratic nations are profoundly influenced by TV broadcasting, reporting, and review. More than any other constituent element, it determines the current state and future prospects of democratic societies.

> After Eisenhower's two [electoral] victories . . . campaigns were dominated not by the old political bosses but by the new political "consultants", who applied the techniques of television advertising and wartime propaganda to . . . "the great game of politics", [which], like baseball, was played increasingly on artificial turf. Trickery, charges of intemperance, infidelity, and even mental instability could now be spread not merely to local audiences, but to vast television watchers nationwide. Money to buy expensive time on the networks was increasingly solicited from special interest groups. . . .
>
> The balance of power shifted during the communications revolution in favor of the politicians who made and manipulated the news. Their pollsters told them what the people wanted to hear and what they didn't want to hear. Their photographers and make-up artists coached them in the most favorable camera angles. Their researchers showed them how to doctor facts. They had speech-writers and even gag-writers who produced the best speeches money can buy, and these were read out by the candidates from invisible screens. Finally, their campaign managers and tour direc-

> tors mapped out their itineraries, picked their sympathetic audiences and flag-waving backgrounds, and arranged for them to avoid, whenever possible, the nosy questions of the press.[37]

Since the built-in dynamic of television is "entertainment", more and more athletic events, which were once broadcast with a single announcer and no concocted fanfare, are now "treated" as "shows" with several commentators, background information, and other appendages designed to further entertain the viewer and fill in any silent or idle periods in the action. The procedural conduct of athletics and other organized activity is often altered to favor TV coverage. Increasingly, as noted previously, "normal" entertainment on television consists of movies and programs which incorporate extensive violence, gun play, sex, and mayhem. Many local news broadcasts select events that are dramatic and titillating, with correspondingly less news which is not exciting but is important enough to warrant coverage. Crime tends to dominate local TV news.

> For seven hours daily—[the station] recycles its tableau of crime highlights, breathless Hollywood gossip, the requisite sports and weather, and anti-Castro editorializing . . . spices things up with its lightning delivery, grainy re-enactments in slow-motion . . . odd camera angles and flashy computer graphics . . . frenetic, electronic music created by the station's full-time composer. Anchors and reporters play along: The women wear sequined clothes and big earrings suitable for an evening gala; the men's ties are bold and bright.[38]

Unintentionally or intentionally television is expanding its entertainment and reportive activities to include direct participation in public and private affairs. By repeatedly focusing on an aspect of the news which impresses viewers emotionally, TV can generate collective reaction so strong that it forces formulation or change of public or private policy. Unfortunately, the response engendered may be neither the best nor appropriate. Analysis of different conclusions and alternate courses of action rarely occurs on TV. By bringing particular people together on television programs the medium encourages or forces a dialogue which normally takes place in official negotiations or private discussion. What is said and suggested publicly on TV before hundreds of thousands or millions of viewers can hardly be denied later or reversed without explanation. It must be taken into account in any subsequent consultations. Television is acting more and more as a means of direct and semiofficial discussion, collective conclusion, and decision. Government officials and business leaders appear on TV programs to explain or justify their actions and activities. Heads-of-state use the medium for many purposes. Political candidates appear as often as possible to become better known or to promote their views, elected representatives to vindicate their performance in office. It is the best way of communicating with the mass of people, immediately and effectively. It can shape policy and induce action. It can operate to discuss, negotiate, and resolve significant societal problems.

> The television camera is as blunt as it is powerful; it is a prisoner of its own immediacy. The pictures from Somalia cry out that something must be done. . . . [It is] the inbuilt, inescapable strength and limitation of the medium that the camera carries the day. Even as the pictures prepare viewers for action, they overwhelm analysis. . . . The medium can be and will be used to whip up popular emotions.[39]

> The decision to move a sizable American military contingent into Somalia was probably the furthest thing from President Bush's mind, but he had to act, because of the pictures on television, pictures that are truly heart breaking.[40]

> When scenes of families stranded on rooftops appear on the nightly news for five days running, nothing can stop Congress from picking up the tab.[41]

As noted earlier in this book, communication has been the critical element in the functioning of all animate communities since their evolutionary beginning millions of years ago. It determines more than any other component the current condition and prospects of society. The above brief review of television as it is functioning in the United States today indicates its pervasive impact on activities and attitudes throughout the nation. As telecomputing develops dramatically during the next ten to twenty years, this means of communication will become ever more critical. The nature and success of planning as an inherent element of human behavior will depend on the nature and extent of mass communication—especially interactive telecomputing—since both are predominant forces in society.

> We live in a media era in which television, radio, movies, and the print media have a more immediate and pervasive influence than any other institutions in society. More powerful than the government, the church, educational institutions, or even the family, the mass media have become the Big Brother that George Orwell anticipated.[42]

Those who employ and view television for particular purposes are well aware of one or several of its multiple uses and impacts. Politicians know that nowadays election and re-election require exposure on TV. Large businesses advertise on TV to increase sales, affect consumer attitudes, and otherwise produce results beneficial to their interests. Scientists and scholars in general are finding that interactive telecomputer networks enable them to communicate directly and almost immediately with others working in their field or one related to it; to tap the vast resources of libraries, data banks, and other depositories of information; to contact experts of almost any kind nearby or far away. Educators are learning that television and computer screens can be used to present and explain some subjects and events more effectively than in any other way. Individuals and organizations seek public recognition, publicity of some sort, or favorable response to a specific objective or cause. Ordinary TV viewers are familiar with the movies, special programs, sports and other events which are broadcast for their entertainment and favorable reaction to accompanying advertising. Managers and administrators know the importance of the computer in almost every organizational operation. It is increasingly employed in household affairs. Those who own or control television stations, networks, or popular TV programs know the potential profit, political power, or other influence which can be derived.

What is not yet recognized or acknowledged is the full impact on society of the different uses of television. Broadcasters judge the contents and effects of their programs in terms of their self-interests. They do not believe there can be any negative societal effects, and any claims to the contrary are ignored or disclaimed. The employment of TV for a particular purpose is judged by its contribution to the attainment of that purpose, more than any lasting impact on society at large. How do we know for certain that it affects social behavior generally? According to TV users, there is no indisputable evidence that violence on television relates to individual aggressiveness. Furthermore it is not important compared with many other considerations to be taken into account. Scheduling frequent reruns of old movies is a constructive use of TV-time as long as audience ratings are maintained. Selection of the most dramatic news events for broadcast and their repetition on successive newscasts conforms to the emotional predispositions of most TV viewers, and their desire to be entertained as much or more than they want to be informed. Broadcasting pseudo-events is justified to maintain a "level playing field" among competitors using manipulative techniques of emphasis or enhancement. Treating sports and many other events as shows attracts and interests viewers who would not watch without the added entertainment. Owners and operators of TV stations are best equipped to decide what proportion of TV time can be devoted to advertising, promotional announcements, and content other than that of the primary program. Broadcasters should determine the falsehood in advertising and the manipulation of program content they will disseminate over the air. Minimum government intervention in private enterprise produces optimal results for television owners and operators, individual viewers, and society at large.

Little thought has been given to the role and functioning of the mass media as a societal system which responds to public preferences and performs positively in the general public interest. The way television is conducted in the United States today presumes that commercial competition among TV stations and other controlling forces produces the best results for everyone concerned and for society as a whole. There is serious question, however, if an adversarial system controlled by private enterprise can serve the general public interest and also maximize private profit. The negative aspects of the existing system noted previously are not likely to change by themselves: excessive violence, sexuality, and emotionalism; poor quality and overly repetitive programming; frequent use of pseudo-events; manipulation of visual images and sound effects; and overaggressive and intrusive reporting. The built-in dynamics of the competitive system seeking ever higher audience ratings suggest that these undesirable practices will become progressively worse. Advertising occupies an increasing percentage of broadcast time.

It is not necessary to accept the opinion of a former U.S. Federal Communications Commissioner that television is a "vast wasteland" to know that it could be far better than it is. Besides reversing harmful practices, desirable features and services not now available can be initiated: diverse and accurate news coverage; important public announcements and explanations of many kinds; expository and educational programs in the public interest; and entertainment which is constructive for both the individual and society, and not completely dependent on advertising or other promotional income. Some of the arguments supporting the present television system will be modified or reinterpreted as telecomputing becomes a force so pervasive in human affairs that entertainment becomes only one of its many functions.

GOVERNMENT

There can be no question that the American people are disillusioned with their government. In their judgment—expressed in public opinion surveys, individual interviews, on television and radio programs, and in newspapers—the system of representative government in the United States is not working well. And the body politic is beginning to vote accordingly.

> Voters everywhere are fed up, polls show. They are annoyed by leaders who appear small at a time when the problems facing them are big. They are disgusted with finding indecision and corruption when they look for direction. And it is not just individual politicians who are the targets of public frustration: In places like Japan and Italy, the whole political system is being called into question. "We are witnessing a crisis of representative democracy," says former French President Valéry Giscard d'Estaing.[43]

Special Interests

In the United States the reasons for this disillusionment in the capabilities and character of the political leaders we elect, and our lack of confidence in our nation's prospects which it brings about, are well known and widely discussed. People are aware that our elected officials represent special interests more than those of the electorate as a whole, private or personal concerns more than the public welfare, their particular jurisdictions more than the national and societal interest. The increasing cost of election and re-election requires large campaign funds obtained for the most part from special interests, which expect immediate access to their representative and some form of tangible return: a favorable vote on specific legislation; political support on an issue; modification or interpretation of a rule or regulation they would like to see changed; or some other action beneficial to the special interest.

> Candidates for the House and Senate spent more than two-thirds of a billion dollars on their 1992 election campaigns, 52% more than was spent in the 1990 legislative races. . . . Below the surface of those numbers is the specter of enormously increased special-interest influence. That's where the cash came from, from both PACs [political action committees] and large individual contributions.[44]

These developments have transformed most elected representatives from the original concept of community leaders serving part-time in government for a limited period, to permanent incumbents of their political post because of the high cost of election and the desire of special interests to retain them in their position where they can be helpful. Holding political office has become for many a professional occupation and a sinecure, rather than a time of temporary public service for those able to support themselves in some other way. Since politicians place re-election above all else, they avoid controversial issues, however important, as long as possible for fear of alienating their electorate and thereby threatening their re-election; "management by crisis" is the result. Crucial matters are postponed until something must be done to prevent catastrophe. By this time the difficulties and cost of remedial action are much greater, and there is always the possibility it may be too late to take effective action.

Corruption

Although mild forms of corruption are endemic in human affairs, the image of our elected representatives has been seriously tarnished in recent years by widely publicized corruption at all levels of government. Many legislators have been indicted, convicted, or forced to resign because they could not sucessfully refute allegations. The public concludes that very likely more are guilty than are caught. A large number engage in the basic immorality of representing special interests rather than the best interests of the electorate. Some carry over excess campaign funds with them into voluntary or forced retirement, which was not the intent of the donors unless they were paying for services already rendered. A series of scandals have been exposed by investigative reporting, official inquiry, or inadvertent disclosure. Witness the improper use of the congressional post office and other perquisites by senators and representatives; bribes and payoffs of state legislators for favorable votes, videotaped for all to see on TV nightly news; and donations to the campaign funds of some local government officials, predicated on a zone change, waiver from a legislative requirement or restriction, or some other helpful action. Many of those seeking elective office engage in innuendo, half-truths, and downright falsehoods in their public statements and advertising. Moral disintegration progresses as each candidate concludes that whatever he does is justified because his opponent has adopted the same tactic. Unfortunately, in today's political climate, the candidate with the most money to spend is likely to win, since his or her pronouncements are publicized most frequently, without the public being aware of any questionable claims or outright misrepresentations.

Many politicians may play games with legislation which are morally difficult to justify. To please some group among their electorate, they sponsor legislation desired by the group, knowing that it has no chance of being enacted. In this way they can claim credit for trying to satisfy different political factions and interests, although they would not have supported the legislation had it a chance of success. Besides the questionable morality of such deception, this practice clogs the calendar of the legislature and wastes time and money when there is never enough of both for important bills with considerable support. This is one of the reasons thousands of laws are introduced every year in many legislatures, but only a small fraction of them are enacted. Also, for some sixty years until very recently, the use of "discharge petitions" in the U.S. House of Representatives has allowed members to block legislation in secret while supporting it in public.

Inefficiency

In general, legislatures tend to become more complex and more inefficient in their operations. Congress is certainly an example.

> It's no secret that the U.S. Congress is inefficient. . . . Thirty committees and . . . 77 subcommittees picked at pieces of last year's defense budget. Forty committees and subcommittees demand a say in energy legislation. The original Clean Air Act covered a page and a half; the latest renewal filled 313 pages. . . . All told there are 300 full committees and subcommittees. To justify their existence, they generate ideas for legislation. In the 101st Congress, 6,973 bills were introduced; barely 200 became law.[45]

On the average, each U.S. senator is a member of eleven committees and subcommittees, every representative seven committees and subcommittees. There are not enough hours in the day and the night to perform effectively in so many assignments. Their subjective jurisdiction often overlaps, so that proposed legislation and other matters must be considered by as many as four or five different committees holding separate hearings. This needlessly complicates and delays the work of these committees and Congress, and probably results in diluted or confused results.

Operating tactics or inefficiencies can thwart the best intentions of members of Congress. They may receive legislation just before a final floor vote is scheduled. They do not have time to absorb the contents of the bill and its last-minute changes and amendments, and they are, therefore, in many cases voting blind. As one member of Congress remarked about the situation described immediately below: "Not one member knows what he's voting on today!"

> Most of them didn't get a chance to look at the 3,000 page [budget] plan before they approved it. . . . To pass judgment on $496 billion in taxes and spending cuts . . . they would have had to review more than $688 million of spending proposal every minute [in the 12 hours available between its publication in the Congressional Record and the final vote].[46]

This delay, which prevents some members from performing as well as they would like, makes it much easier for surreptitious alterations to pass through undetected. Congressional rules and procedures have been honed to perfection over the years to allow every member to obtain for purely political purposes some "pork" for his or her constituency, by subtle parliamentary maneuvers, devious procedural devices, amendments, last-minute changes, or delays in legislation. If it cannot be done before the law is enacted, there is often an opportunity to insert or modify a rule or regulation required to effectuate the law so that it favors a hometown constituent or campaign fund contributor. Or by attaching a rider to major legislation that cannot be delayed and will be enacted by a legislative majority and signed by the president, because there is a deadline or because so much time and effort have been expended on an excellent law: except for the parasitic rider which would not be approved by itself. To engage in such tactics and for the legislature to allow them is irresponsible, underhanded, and hardly conducive to efficient operations. To expect legislatures, however, to set an example of straightforward and efficient procedures is to deny the nature of the political human animal. But the modus operandi which has evolved over the years by Congress guarantees inefficiency if not functional gridlock.

There is serious question whether a governing body of 535 individuals can operate effectively. Besides the problems presented by its overall size, some of its committees have as many as thirty or forty members. This size almost ensures that members will concentrate on the prestige, personal advantages, and political benefits to be derived from membership on the committee, rather than attempting to resolve common problems at hand requiring painstaking collective effort by many people. The problem of congressional size is compounded by the fact that it exists because our constitutional structure separates the nation into fifty states, each with its elected representatives, cherished history and ambitions, "state's rights", and agenda for legislative and other action. There is only secondary interest in national and international affairs unless they affect the state.

> American policies are driven by the efforts of particular interests and regions to frustrate national goals and policies; it is hard to imagine legislators who have prospered under such a system changing their ways and adopting a national, let alone a global perspective.[47]

But technological advances and economic developments indicate clearly that our primary problems must be addressed at national and international levels. How to achieve the required integration of attitude, consideration, planning, and constructive action among the elected representatives of fifty different states is certainly a foremost challenge of our time.

Partisanship

Constructive action is made all the more difficult by political partisanship, which divides legislators into opposing camps concentrating on the next elections rather than bipartisan effort and decisive action in the national and societal best interest. Except in dire emergencies, constructive bipartisanship appears less and less likely as campaign costs and the other requirements for election to public office intensify partisan rivalry. It is the most critical issues before Congress that are apt to become embroiled in partisan battle, with the lowest common denominator or legislative deadlock the probable result. At times, states in a geographical region or dispersed throughout the nation but with a common self-interest may combine to form a powerful politically partisan force. But this is not likely to contribute much to the national cohesion of effort so badly needed. When legislative deadlock occurs on issues that are not national emergencies but Congress believes the situation demands action, a special commission is sometimes appointed to study the issue and decide what should be done. Congress agrees beforehand to accept or reject the recommendation in its entirety without change: tacit admission that as it is presently constituted and operates Congress cannot act impartially on certain of the nation's most important needs.

Parochialism

The parochial view of Congress reflected in many of its characteristics noted in preceding paragraphs accounts for its reluctance to address national and international problems and prospects. Even more important, the needs of society as an organic entity receive little attention. It is presumed that if the immediate political, economic, and social problems are addressed, societal requirements and needs are met. This is an illusion. Rational planning and constructive action to resolve major problems are impeded by our predilection to place self-interest above all else, to react emotionally rather than rationally to difficulties that must be surmounted, and our reluctance to acknowledge disturbing realities. We are prone to false hopes, prejudices and intolerance, violence, and superstitions and mythical beliefs. Most of these are products of our primitive selves. They direct our reactions and actions as much or more as our rational thoughts and civilized behavior. Our parochialism is a geographical rather than substantive justification for political partisanship.

Sooner or later, however, the essential requirements of our societal existence must be met. For example, we cannot continue fouling our environment indefinitely without threatening our survival as a species. We cannot tolerate social disruption to the point of societal disintegration. We cannot forever spend beyond our capability to produce without accumulating a burden of debt which becomes socioeconomically intolerable and could eventually destroy the existing society. We cannot disregard communications—the most critical element of society—until they operate as a destructive rather than a constructive force in society. Above all, we can no longer believe that evolutionary forces or our automatic instinctive responses can guide us successfully in a world shaped increasingly by scientific and technological advances. We must recognize that planning is essential for societal survival and success, that it must be longer range because many of the vital forces of society function gradually and inevitably over a period of many years. The human animal and his emotions change not much from age to age. He must change now or he faces absolute complete destruction and maybe the insect age or an atmosphereless plant will succeed him.[48]

Difficulties of Democracy

Representative democracy as a form of government is a recent arrival on the human scene. Throughout history it has been the great exception rather than the rule. Even with the breakup of the Soviet Union in the early 1990s and shifts to more democratic governments in other countries, only one-quarter of the world population lives in free societies in 1993. Almost one-half live in countries with governmental systems that are only partly free, and almost one-third live under totalitarian regimes: controlled by dictatorships, military juntas, or feudal kings. Some 75% of the global population of about five and one-half billion people live under governments that violate human rights as defined in the Universal Declaration of Human Rights.[49]

These facts confirm the difficulties of establishing and maintaining democratic societies that require the populace to exercise the initiative or at least the willingness to participate in its electoral and representative procedures, to choose among alternatives that are not available in autocratic regimes but may not be missed if people are willing to follow the leader. People have a built-in tendency to accept or prefer leadership, which we accepted from our parents and may or may not continue to accept or prefer as adults. Our predecessors in primitive communities depended on their leaders to provide the experience and judgment required for survival, and to pass on the accumulated knowledge of the community to the next generation by word of mouth before the advent of writing.

Democratic societies are more active and difficult to manage than those whose members are willing or forced to accept a more passive role of concurrence. They are also likely to be more complex for the individual because his involvement in determining policies and evaluating political decisions is procedurally more complicated than accepting the mandatory directives of a single authority. In wartime, democracy yields most individual freedoms to the autocratic direction and control of the military system. For the victor and to a lesser extent the vanquished the operational advantages of centralized and firm managerial control are demonstrated. Since the military function in peacetime as well as during wars which occur frequently, the system is at hand to be observed and possibly applied in whole or in part in civil government.

Underlying these speculations is the fact that autocratic societies differ in the nature and extent of centralized control and the democratic freedoms that are violated. And societies with democratic systems of government differ to the extent they nonetheless disregard some human rights. While democracy is a concept and political reality which can vary considerably in its form and degree of development, "eternal vigilance" is necessary to maintain and improve the process. To deserve this vigilance, democracy must function effectively enough to preserve and improve the society that practices it.

Unless the federal government resolves the problems of directive leadership noted in previous pages, some form of governmental authority will be established to cut the Gordian knot of legislative deadlock, unwillingness to act, or managerial ineptitude.

> Americans have been sold on the notion that government is a hopeless instrument for solving problems, and from that idea we have been propelled into a prolonged state of denial about conditions, such as urban ghettos and homelessness, for which the marketplace holds no plausible remedies.[50]

Where this will lead politically is anybody's guess, but it must involve some loss of personal preference or choice, at least temporarily. Political leadership can no longer choose not to act decisively on critical problems until a societal crisis develops. Emergencies have always justified postponing existing procedures or requirements which would delay or prevent recovery, taking unusual or unprecedented actions to relieve the crisis condition. A special executive authority, commission, or agency may be designated or created to plan and administer the activities intended to restore normal conditions. For Congress there is the precedent, referred to above, of appointing a special commission to act in its behalf and determine what it should do to resolve crucial matters it cannot or will not tackle.

Crisis Conditions

A case can be made that the United States is approaching a state of emergency in 1993 as a result of escalating violence, crime, gang warfare, and civil unrest throughout the nation; increasing drug and alcohol addiction; serious educational deficiencies for one-half the adult population; and dissolution of the traditional family unit as an individually supportive and socially stabilizing element.

> The traditional American family has declined so far in New York City that married couples with their own children now constitute only one in six households. . . . Fully one in four whites do not live in family households at all. . . . And one in five households are headed by a woman with no husband present.[51]

The country has a growing underclass of disadvantaged citizens and a body of permanently unemployed and unemployable people; and an economically ruinous national debt out of control. This is a depressing list of super-serious problems. They are disclaimed by some, denied or disregarded by others, but they cannot be refuted. They exist. The need for a "strong man" to slow down and in time reverse these dire developments will be championed by those so inclined. The situation as it exists now is a constant threat to democratic government.

The most serious deficiencies of representative government in the United States are at the federal level, somewhat less at the state level, and least in local government. It appears that the further government is spatially separated from the electorate it serves, the worse its functional problems. Local governments are situated within their political jurisdiction. Local legislatures are under the watchful eye of the voters who are familiar with the local scene and its particular problems. Poor performance and misbehavior can and do occur at the local level, but they are usually less severe and certainly less all-encompassing and impactful than when they occur in a state capitol or in Washington, D.C. It is the national government that has the ultimate responsibility and authority to shape the affairs of the nation and society.

As our society becomes more complex and is affected more and more by scientific, technological, and international economic developments, the critical issues become broader in scope and the crucial decisions must be made at the national level. They cannot be addressed separately and successfully by fifty different states and thousands of local governments. Within the overarching policies and actions of the national government, state and local authorities fine-tune their implementation of federal prescriptions to fit their local needs. Those who engage in the political game of bashing the federal government and calling for its drastic reduction in size and function, ignore the realities of national needs, problems, and the world today as it is clearly developing. With some five million employees—including the U.S. Postal Service and the military services—and thirty thousand field officers all told, the federal government is oversized and certainly not as efficient as it should be. But it provides the essential leadership for the nation. The all-important concern is not how much it can be shrunk, but how it can be made to operate effectively and successfully perform its essential functions in society.

COMMUNICATION AND GOVERNMENT

Broadly defined, communication includes television, telephone, radio, the written word, the human voice and gestures, movies, videotapes, computers, vehicles, and other means of maintaining contact among humans. As noted earlier in this book, the most vital of these will coalesce into the telecomputer network which will serve as the main means of personal and organizational communication, with momentous consequences for individuals and society. Television will be the element in this amalgam affecting the mass of people most directly and profoundly. In turn, what affects television is significant with respect to communication in general and its relation to society.

Dynamics of Television

It is important to recognize the built-in dynamics of television, brought about by the fierce competition for superior audience ratings. They determine what appears on the TV screen, and they explain the progressive changes in its treatment and content which occur. An awareness of these intrinsic forces is essential to understanding the nature and functioning of the medium.

They are illustrated in the development of network broadcasting of professional and college football games. What once involved small TV audiences and small sums of money, now involve millions of viewers and hundreds of millions of dollars. Super Bowl XXVII in 1993 attracted a record television audience of 133.4 million viewers for more than three hours nonstop. Advertisers spent $850,000 for thirty-second spots during the game. Many professional players receive salary contracts in the millions of dollars. Super Bowls comprise nine of television's most watched programs.[52] They are in fact mammoth "shows". As the senior announcer in a network football broadcasting crew admitted: "I'll be honest with you, show business is a big part of our business." Television revenues from several college football games support the entire athletic program of some universities.

In the beginning football games were broadcast with a single announcer and commentator, and a small crew of technicians. If not inconspicuous, advertising was a minor interruption. Progressively over time, the number of announcers of a single game has multiplied to three or even more, often with additional interviewers down on the field talking to people they entice to the portable camera and microphone. There is no lack of interviews since most people are attracted to TV for the psychological satisfaction of being seen "on camera" and/or the commercial value of the publicity it provides. To avoid the sin of silence lasting more than a few seconds, some announcer is declaiming continuously during the prolonged broadcast period or advertisements are occupying the eyes and ears of the listener. Often the spiel is so fast and the information so overconcentrated that much of it is unintelligible: continuous artificial sound rather than comprehensive content. The scores of other games underway elsewhere are announced or interjected as graphical inserts at the bottom of the TV screen. During half-time, announcers may ruminate on the game, interview guests in the broadcast booth, or run videotapes of prior interviews with players and their families, or of episodes relating in some way to the game or to football. They may even interview players at home who are "holding out" from signing a contract and are therefore absent from the game, thereby intruding indirectly into the contract negotiating process between the player and team management.

The time devoted to advertising in one form or another is increasing. Most recently "self-advertising" has been introduced, advising the viewer of forthcoming programs on the TV station he is watching which he should not miss by turning to another channel. Advertising of beer is allowed although alcoholism is a major social problem for the nation, for a considerable number of the spectators in the stadium, and for some of the players on the field. Time-outs and other interruptions in the game are arranged to fit television coverage and commercial advertising breaks. Officials announce their rulings to the TV camera, not to the spectators in the stadium. The advertising blimp hovers overhead, providing a few camera shots of the playing field and stadium below in the distance. Stadiums have been enlarged and new ones built primarily for football, including the "luxury boxes" for seasonal lease to corporations and wealthy people wishing an enclosed space and ample room from which to view the game in relaxed comfort: an important source of additional income for the stadium owner. In some stadiums TV screens display advertising and scenes relating to the game under way.

In the early days of television, footballers and spectators paid little or no attention to the TV camera recording the game. Nowadays, not only do many professional and some college players engage in some form of antic after they have scored, but any member of the team may posture and perform for the spectators and TV audience after "sacking" the opposing quarterback or engaging in any other play in a way he believes merits such display. The referees do not restrict this increasing personal exhibitionism.

With their heavily padded uniforms, helmets with face masks, and posturing, professional football players could be mistaken for gladiators performing in the Coliseum in ancient Rome. Spectators now include people dressed up in all sorts of costumes, bearing signs, or otherwise bedecked to express themselves or attract attention. This trend toward gladiator-like entertainment has produced a TV program bearing the same name. Professional "wrestling" matches broadcast on television are pure exhibitionist theater, thoroughly rehearsed beforehand to simulate hostility, violence, and total disdain for any restraining rules or regulations. Wrestling spectators respond accordingly for that is what they come to see and experience with vicarious emotions. Rather than the customary cheers, boos, and epithets today, in the future winning or losing may initiate the thumbs-up of approval or the thumbs-down of disapproval introduced by Caesar Augustus to decide whether a surviving gladiator should live or be killed. Football players in the United States do not yet engage in life or death combat, but the injuries they sustain are increasing.

If this brief description of developments in the televised broadcasting of professional football in the United States is surprising or even disturbing, it is not because of any exaggeration or misstatement of fact but because so many characteristics of the system are concentrated in a few paragraphs. Football TV programs are an economic force involving directly and indirectly billions of dollars, hundreds of thousands of people, hundreds of enterprises participating in one way or another, and large actual or potential profits. They are a significant element in the national economy and export sales abroad. They entertain millions of viewers. They serve as an emotional outlet or distraction for hundreds of thousands of people who are unemployed, disadvantaged, or just plain bored or at loose ends. Professional football games are somewhat like the gladiatorial combats, chariot races, and other spectacles produced in ancient Rome to entertain and divert from civil unrest or insurrection the potential mob of dispossessed people, slaves, captives, and immigrant non-citizens.

Professional football broadcasting also demonstrates the escalatory force built into competitive television characterized by more and more extraneous content, exhibitionism, and whatever manipulation or additional features will increase or at least maintain existing audience ratings. Football occupies a substantial block of available television time. It is pure entertainment, but it also provides role models for young people of exemplary individual and team capabilities and behavior. Unfortunately, professional football players and semiprofessional college athletes are not the role models they once were. Increasing exhibitionism, excessive violence on the field, drug addiction, illegal use of steroids, scandals, misbehavior, and widely publicized disputes have tarnished the image of professional football players and their usefulness as role models for young people.

The facts of football broadcasting and the questions they raise apply to other TV programs. Soap operas may not have as much violence but they are replete with sex. To attract viewers, the old movies selected for airing are filled with violence, heavy with sex, or contain other intensely emotional content. Even the fifteen-second announcements telling viewers when these films will be broadcast emphasize emotional content. The movies most frequently rebroadcast are those that disturb most adults because of their content, have the worst effects on children, and are most stimulating to young gang members and potential delinquents to go forth and do likewise. Network news programs also select, emphasize, and repeat most often the information and events with the most dramatic content.

Questions to be Answered

This dynamic of progressive dramatization raises many questions. How much of the day and night should be devoted to entertainment? What sort of entertainment? Should TV broadcast public announcements, explain conditions and situations of public concern, and present educational programs on matters of general public interest? What is its responsibility with respect to the portrayal of violence and other socially disruptive or destructive actions? To what extent should it be a vehicle to incite, encourage, distress, disturb, mislead, or otherwise affect most viewers? Should explicit sex be shown or simulated on television? Should TV broadcast far and wide how criminal acts can be carried out successfully without detection, simulate enthusiastic applause when none occurred, or alter scenes or events to produce false images? Are there certain behavioral or environmental requirements for societal survival and advancement which should be treated in TV programs and otherwise called to public attention by this primary means of communication?

If communication is the most crucial element in society and government by definition and of necessity must provide overall leadership, they must be considered together. What is the role of government with respect to telecomputing as it gradually integrates television, radio, newspapers, personal computers, and perhaps telephones into a single unified means of providing every household with current information, services, entertainment, educational programs, and access to a vast and ever-increasing body of information maintained in many repositories not only in the United States but around the world? We are considering a system that is not only the main means of personal and societal communication within the United States, but also a primary part of the global system of contact and intercommunication which is developing. It is as important and necessary for the federal government to participate actively in this system as it is for it to be involved with monetary matters, treaties and agreements between countries, financial and business operations comprising the national economy, political and social developments affecting public safety and welfare, and other essential elements of national and global existence. If government does not generally direct communication, it will in fact if not officially abrogate its responsibility for societal leadership to whatever organization or individual assumes this directive control.

What is the function of a national government with respect to communication? First and foremost, can it function successfully? If not, what is needed to achieve the requisite level of performance? Should it play an active role in what appears and does not appear on TV? Should TV stations be owned and operated by individuals, private enterprises, or other institutions, organizations, associations, or groups of people under the jurisdiction of the Federal Communications Commission? Is there a limit to the number of television and radio stations, newspapers, computer networks, and telephone systems that an individual or organization can own or control within the United States? What standards, if any, should be established for all broadcasting and utilization of computer networks? Who should control the use or assignment of broadcast microwave frequencies within the airspace of the United States? Who is responsible for the accuracy of what is broadcast and disseminated over telecomputer networks? Who is to prevent illegal use or intentional disruption of the communication system?

> Companies . . . have found their phone systems shut down by voice-mail vandals who clogged the systems so nothing more could fit in. Hackers sometimes occupy a vacant corporate voice-mailbox and use it to post messages to other hackers. In some cases phone thieves have even managed to go from voice-mailboxes into outbound calling, racking up thousands of dollars of international calls.[53]

These fundamental questions must be asked and answered by the federal government which has final responsibility for the welfare of the nation.

COMMUNICATION AND EDUCATION

Government and television are both involved in resolving the serious educational problem facing the United States today. Those concerned with public education have known for years that it was not keeping up with the educational requirements of the marketplace. Toward the end of 1993, the nation learned that

> Nearly half of adult Americans (91 million people) have such weak reading and math skills that they were unable to perform tasks any more difficult than filling out a bank deposit slip or locating an intersection on a street map.[54]

> A large majority of children can't even grasp the basic meaning of what they read. . . . Students who watched more than six hours of television a night had much lower reading scores than [those who watched three hours or less].[55]

The implications for the future of growing illiteracy in the United States can hardly be exaggerated. The productivity and economic health of the nation are linked with the educational level of the population, especially in the technically complex and globally competitive world of today. Greater background knowledge and skills are required for people to function successfully in society as its operational systems are made more complex by advances in science and technology. The nation that does not educate its children and its adult population to keep up with these changes will gradually deteriorate internally, with mounting social problems and eventual civil unrest. In time, it will lose out economically and politically to other countries with better educated and more productive work forces.

As matters now stand, educational deficiencies threaten our welfare, social stability, cultural advancement, our capability to add to the body of knowledge we employ in all our operations, and to absorb and use advanced knowledge developed by others. There is the increasing danger of a society fractured not only by extreme differences between the economic haves and have-nots, but also between the educated, inadequately educated, and uneducated. This division creates a socially explosive mixture in today's world of exposure, disclosure, and emotional reaction produced by the mass media of communication, which becomes all the more disruptive as our society becomes culturally and ethnically more diverse. Were science fiction speculations to be realized, resulting in highly automated robotic systems of production with few human participants, more people in a growing population would need education to engage in the service activities, cultural endeavors, and intellectual self-advancement which would occupy their time. Those without education would have to rely on sports and other entertainment live or on TV to avoid disabling boredom and disillusionment which could lead to active unrest.

Upgrading American education is a tremendous undertaking. Ninety-one million of our adult population are now rated as functionally illiterate. Millions of children and adolescents are not receiving the education they need to perform successfully in the world they will enter as adults. As now constituted, the public school system in the United States cannot handle the number of people in need of at least minimum education, nor will it on its own develop and incorporate the methods of instruction that are required to teach a large segment of the middle class who have little education, and the totally unmotivated, the poor, and the multiply disadvantaged "underclass". More money is needed now just to restore deteriorated school buildings, increase teachers' salaries, and provide needed equipment and other instructional support for the existing system. When public schools are upgraded, they will still educate only part of the much larger group that needs remedial education. Colleges and universities will continue to educate a limited number of undergraduates and graduate students provided enough financial help is awarded to offset the rising cost of tuition and living expenses, and if extraneous courses are foregone in favor of those that cover the basic knowledge that is a foundation for an informed life, substantive specialization if desired, and constructive citizenship.

Eliminating illiteracy in the United States requires a new educational system employing telecomputers and a national communication network. The teacher is the unseen person who has organized the content of what is seen on the TV screen, and will monitor the student's performance by surrogate intelligence incorporated in the computer program or in person as required. The instructor could introduce most students to the telecomputerized educational program in person, and be available during the course as needed. TV teachers will be superior to most of those performing in conventional classrooms because they have been identified as the best, and the best of several of their presentations are selected for television instruction.

Telecomputer programs would be designed to attract and motivate those needing remedial education. If as much time, energy, money, and talent are devoted to educational telecomputer programs as are expended on commercial advertising, we can achieve impressive educational results. Experience indicates that most children can be intrigued into learning by associating the educational content with a computer game or subject matter they like to watch. Adults with little educational motivation can be attracted by associating the remedial educational content with a personal interest of theirs or through some routine activity with which they are familiar, such as shopping at the supermarkets, driving an automobile, or preparing a meal. Various experiences and subjects, some one of which is familiar or attractive to most people, would be selected to usher in the remedial educational content. An increasing number of educational programs are in fact being composed for the computer. If we advertise on TV and conduct all sorts of operations on a computer, we can combine both to educate people to literacy. A beginning is being made with the "distant learning" programs of the Public Television Corporation. The main obstacles are traditionalism, vested interests in the prevailing educational system, and unfamiliarity with the telecomputer technology and the potentialities of skillful computer programming.

The telecomputing system must be available twenty-four hours a day at home, in a special classroom, anywhere a standard or portable telecomputer is available. Progress will be monitored, measured, and recorded by questions, tests, and other means incorporated in the program. Those needing but resisting remedial education would be required to enroll, as high-school students are supposed to do today. Acquiring minimum education would be linked with something the prospective student needs or desires, perhaps a driver's license, credit card, citizenship, or whatever can be reasonably related to an individual's literacy. The motivation to undertake and continue the process of remedial education will be built into the telecomputer program. As the years go by, it is likely that this form of televised education will comprise an increasing part of an improved public school system.

Ironically, a convincing reason for such a system was provided inadvertently by the U.S. Secretary of Education, who proclaimed with reference to children: "If parents turn off their television sets, we will transform the nation."[56] Children do indeed watch TV for hours, often almost mesmerized by the medium. Instead of trying to persuade parents to limit television viewing by their children as the Secretary suggests—an impractical, impossible, or unpleasant task in most instances—their fascination with the TV screen can be used to great educational advantage. It is not the medium that is at fault; it is the content or message that is being transmitted today that justifies limited or very little viewing.

EDUCATION AND GOVERNMENT

Government relates to education in many ways. School boards operate independently within local governmental jurisdictions. They determine the location and type of public school facilities, the nature of the curriculum, and the general teaching methods employed. State governments provide operating funds from state sales taxes and may pressure the local school boards concerning their choice of textbooks, the content of the curriculum, or other controversial subjects. At the national level, the supreme court rules on constitutional issues relating to education; federal funds are provided for special educational programs; and federal departments, independent agencies, and the military services initiate and support research conducted for them by higher educational institutions around the country. In general, the federal government has left management and development of the regular public school system to state governments and local school boards. This has resulted in diversity and large disparities in the quality of public education among the states.

A telecomputer system of remedial education, which will gradually eliminate the critical problem of widespread illiteracy, must be nationwide in its coverage and operations. Fifty state systems with different curricula, standards, and procedures cannot be integrated to provide substantive and legal consistency, credit recognition of each other's educational programs, and comparable societal accomplishment throughout the nation. A common core curriculum is needed for consistent instruction, and uniform measurements and standards of student performance to justify the award of diplomas, certificates confirming technical skills, and academic degrees. The rest of the subject matter would be modified at the local level to fit particular regional conditions.

The overall design of the instructional program would be determined by joint deliberation among all major interests involved, but the final responsibility must rest with the federal government which "has to be watched just as carefully as anybody else. The government makes mistakes and tries to conceal mistakes."[57] A special commission can be appointed or an existing authority designated to develop a core curriculum, monitor the remedial programs, and prepare explanatory reports.

GOVERNMENT AND PLANNING

Planning as practiced in the United States at the end of the twentieth century is described briefly in chapter 1. The process has been an essential element in human existence since its inception. Remarkable progress has been made in our ability to plan and to implement complex systems of many kinds, such as the international commercial air transportation system noted in chapter 1 involving almost every element and aspect of society. At the same time, as would be expected, there have been notable failures of planning as well as successes.[58]

It is the absence of comprehensive planning at the legislative level of government that has the most serious consequences for society. This is not a failure of planning as a process. It has not yet been applied experimentally by legislators in their decision making. There is no reason to suppose that it would not be as significant at this highest governmental level as it has been in other applications. Legislators must organize their activities in order to function individually and operate as an organization. This procedural planning is not the comprehensive planning described in the next chapter which is designed to provide the analytical support legislators need to reach sound conclusions underlying the crucial decisions they must make in the best interest of the people they represent. The two applications are methodically similar, but differ in their objectives, range and depth of analysis, and significance.

Legislators have personal staffs to prepare background information on particular issues. In recent years these supportive staffs have increased in size, collecting material and conducting most of the analytical study and thinking on the subject at hand for the legislator. So much so that lobbyists seeking to influence legislation often contact staff members rather than the legislators themselves who spend most of their time soliciting campaign funds and politicking for re-election. At the federal level there are offices established to assist members of Congress in the following ways reported in their respective statement of operations. The Congressional Budget Office "provides Congress with basic budget data and with analyses of alternative fiscal, budgetary, and programmatic policy issues." The Congressional Research Service of the Library of Congress responds to legislators' requests with "written materials, in-person and telephone briefings and consultations, seminars and institutes, and databases prepared for legislative use." The General Accounting Office audits and evaluates government programs and activities, for the most part in response to congressional requests. "The Controller General has virtually unlimited power to investigate government operations." The Office of Technology Assessment "serves the United States Congress by providing objective analysis of major public policy issues related to scientific and technological change. . . . It draws on the broad technical and professional resources of the private sector." And the regular departments and independent agencies of the federal government are available to provide information and analyses when requested by individual members and committees of Congress. Since these supportive resources deal with particular issues on an ad hoc basis, they do not serve the purpose of comprehensive legislative planning.

What is lacking in legislative decision making is a background of analysis that simulates the essential nature of what is being planned: its history, current condition, and projected future. It must be up-to-date, immediately available for reference; it should indicate how the matter at hand relates to other contemporary concerns, what has been done and committed in the past, the capabilities and limitations of the organism being planned, and the probable consequences of proposed courses of action. For legislators, the organism is the nation, a state, or a locality as a geographical and societal unit, or as an administrative jurisdiction that does not coincide with historically established boundary lines. In comprehensive planning for a business, it is a corporation, partnership, or another entrepreneurial entity. In the military services, it is the unit of command: company, brigade, division, corps, army, or combined forces. Comprehensive planning promotes decisions based on the needs and capabilities of the organism being planned, rather than on personal preferences, self-interest, politics, or consideration of only one or several of the primary elements involved. The type of organization and analysis required for comprehensive planning is discussed in the next chapter.

> Indeed our central government, faced with the most gigantic of planning tasks and with the immediate necessity of preventing the disintegration of society, possesses only the most rudimentary mechanisms for the purpose.[59]

REFERENCES

1. Melville C. Branch, *Planning: Universal Process* (New York: Praeger, 1990), 234 pp.

2. Melville C. Branch, *Comprehensive Planning, General Theory and Principles* (Pacific Palisades, CA: Palisades Publishers, 1983), pp. 81–97.

3. Gina Kolata, "Bacteria Are Found to Thrive on a Rich Social Life," *The New York Times*, 13 October 1992, p. zB5.

4. John Lippman, "The Global Village: How TV is Transforming World Culture and Politics," *Los Angeles Times*, 20 October 1992, p. H-2.

5. Edmund L. Andrews, "Cable Concern Plans to Offer 500 Channels," *The New York Times*, 3 December 1992, p. zA1.

6. Lippman, "The Global Village . . ." above.

7. "Who Will Control TV?" *U.S. News and World Report*, 13 May 1985, p. 60.

8. William J. Broad, "Doing Science on the Network, A Long Way From Gutenberg," *The New York Times*, 18 May 1993, p. zB5. Quotation: Dr. Larry Smear (Director, National Center for Supercomputing Applications, University of Illinois).

9. John Markoff, "Turning the Desktop PC Into a Talk Radio Medium," *The New York Times*, 4 March 1993, p. A2z.

10. Rupert Murdoch (Chief Executive, News Corporation), quoted in Lippman, "The Global Village . . ." above, p. H-10.

11. Rone Tempest, "France Plugs Into Future With Video System," *Los Angeles Times*, 18 April 1993, pp. A11–12.

12. Barnaby J. Feder, "A Model for a U.S. High-Tech Network? Try Iowa," *The New York Times*, 5 March 1993, p. zC1.

13. Steve Lohr, "Electronics Replacing Coaches' Clipboards," *The New York Times*, 5 May 1993, p. zC1.

14. Stephen Kreider Yoder and G. Pascal Zachery, "Digital Media Business Takes Form as a Battle of Complex Alliances," *The Wall Street Journal*, 14 July 1993, p. A1.

15. Diedre Carmody, "At the Biggest Magazines, A Revolution Trickles Up," *The New York Times*, 3 May 1993, p. zC5.

16. Daniel Schoor (Senior News Analyst, National Public Radio), Quotes and Ethics/Essays, *Christian Science Monitor*, 1 June 1993, p. 19.

17. Pierre Salinger (Press Secretary to President John F. Kennedy, currently ABC News, Chief Correspondent in Europe), quoted in Keith Henderson, "An Unsanguine Salinger," *Christian Science Monitor*, 8 June 1993, p. 11.

18. Daniel J. Boorstin, quoted in Michiko Kakatuni, "Virtual Confusion: Time for a Reality Check," *The New York Times*, 25 September 1992, pp. B1–B2.

19. Stephen Engelberg, "A New Breed of Hired Hands Cultivates Grass-Roots Anger," *The New York Times*, 17 March 1993, p. A1.

20. Arthur E. Rowse, "Teary Testimony to Push America Toward War," *World*, 18 October 1992, p. 9.

21. James Madison, quoted in *Project Vote Smart, Center for National Independence in Politics*, Corvallis, Oregon, 1993, p. 1.

22. Ken Auletta, "What Won't They Do?," *New Yorker*, 17 May 1993, pp. 45–46.

23. Jeff Sagansky (President, Entertainment Division, Columbia Broadcasting System), quoted in Gretchen Friesinger, *Harvard Magazine*, May/June 1993, p. 25.

24. James Ragan, quoted in *USC Trojan Family*, Summer 1993, p. 15.

25. Elizabeth Kolbert, "A Broadcast Killing Prompts Debate," *The New York Times*, 22 January 1993, p. A7.

26. Neil Postman (Chairman, Department of Communication Arts, New York University), quoted in Elizabeth Kolbert 25. above.

27. Park Elliot Dietz, M.D. (Clinical Professor of Psychiatry and Behavioral Sciences, School of Medicine, University of California, Los Angeles),

quoted in Dorothy Trainor, "Media Contribute to Crime, Says Forensic Expert," *Psychiatric News*, December 1992, p. 5.

28. Marlise Simons, "A French Mother Fights TV Violence," *The New York Times*, 30 August 1993, p. zA5.

29. Eric Larson, "Libraries of Killers Often Include a Book or Two From Paladin," *The Wall Street Journal*, 6 January 1993, p. A1.

30. Michael Waldholz, "Study of Fear Shows Emotions Can Alter 'Wiring' of the Brain," *The Wall Street Journal*, 29 September 1993, p. A1.

31. James Barron, "Live and In Force: It's Somalia With Brokaw," *The New York Times*, 9 December 1992, p. zA8.

32. Eric Larson, "Attention Shoppers: Don't Look Now but You are Being Tailed," *Smithsonian*, January 1993, p. 71.

33. Laura Bird, "First Advertorials; New Advernewscasts," *The Wall Street Journal*, 24 September 1993, p. B1.

34. Joel Winston (Assistant Director, Division of Advertising Practices, U.S. Federal Communications Commission), *The Wall Street Journal*, 19 June 1990, p. B1.

35. John R. Emshwiller, "Radio Station in Los Angeles Offers Look at Controversial 'Brokered-Time' Niche," *The Wall Street Journal*, 18 April 1988, p. 25.

36. Ken Auletta, "Raiding the Global Village," *New Yorker*, 2 August 1993, p. 25.

37. James Reston (Washington Bureau Chief, Executive Editor, Columnist Emeritus, *The New York Times*), *Deadline: A Memoir* (New York: Random House, 1991), pp. 262, 269–270.

38. Elizabeth Jensen, "Corpses, Blood and Sex Put Miami Station At Top of News Heap," *The Wall Street Journal*, 30 July 1993, pp. 1, 4.

39. Walter Goodman, "Re Somalia: How Much Did TV Shape Policy?," *The New York Times*, 8 December 1992, p. B4z.

40. Bernard Kalb (Former Network Correspondent: Director, Sharenstein Barone Center on Press and Politics, Harvard University), quoted in James Barron, "Live and In Force: It's Somalia With Brokaw," *The New York Times*, 9 December 1992, p. 2z A8.

41. Robert Stevins (School of Government, Harvard University), quoted in Peter Passell, "After the Floods, Seeking a More Comprehensive Rebuilding Policy," *The New York Times*, 2 September 1993, p. C2z.

42. Park Elliot Dietz, M.D., see 27. above.

43. Peter Gumbel, "With Voters Fed Up, World Leaders See Their Popularity Sink," *The Wall Street Journal*, 2 July 1993, p. A1.

44. Michael Wines, "Record $678 Million Was Spent By Candidates for Congress in '92," *The New York Times*, 5 March 1993, p. C18z.

45. Editorial, *The New York Times*, 10 February 1993, p. A18z.

46. Dan Greenberg, "Chaos Theory in Congress," *The New York Times*, 2 September 1993, p. zA15.

47. Alan Ryan, "Twenty-first Century Blues," *New York Review of Books*, 13 May 1993, p. 20.

48. Harry S. Truman (President of the United States, 1945–1953), quoted in David McCullough, *Truman* (New York: Simon & Schuster, 1992), p. 519.

49. Robin Wright, "Defining Heroes and Villains in a World That's Shaded in Gray," *Los Angeles Times*, 28 February 1993, p. M1.
50. Notes and Comment, *New Yorker*, 21 September 1992, p. 27.
51. Sam Roberts, "Study Finds Redefining of Family in New York," *The New York Times*, 20 October 1992, p. B12z.
52. Richard Sandomir, "Super Bowl Registers Biggest Audience," *The New York Times*, 3 February 1993, p. zB9.
53. William M. Buckeley, "Voice Mail May Let Competitors Dial 'E' for Espionage," *The Wall Street Journal*, 28 September 1993, p. B1.
54. "Report Offers More Evidence of Literacy Woes in Schools," *The New York Times*, 16 September 1993, p. zA9.
55. Rochelle Sharpe, "Two-Thirds of Children in U.S. Read Below Their Grade Level," *The Wall Street Journal*, 16 September 1993, p. A11.
56. Ibid.
57. Martin Tolchin, "Disillusioned With Government, Judge is Thorn in Side of U.S. Prosecutors," *The New York Times*, 9 October 1992, p. B10z.
58. Melville C. Branch, *Planning, Universal Process* (New York: Praeger, 1990), pp. 87–98.
59. Rexford G. Tugwell, "The Fourth Power," *Planning and Civic Comment*, Part II, April–June 1939, p. 17.

The making of such plans and programs as may be found necessary to meet the demands of social and economic crises does not require any modification of the broad lines of our governmental system. Our Constitution was designed to be and is broad enough to meet a wide variety of changing situations, economic, social, and political. . . .

Wise planning is based on control of certain strategic points . . . necessary to ensure order, justice, general welfare. It involves continuous reorganization of this system of control points as the function and situation shift from time to time. . . .

At various times the community has found it necessary to deal with landowners, with slavery, with the church, with the Army, with industrial or labor captains, with racial groups, adjusting bureaucratic control points to meet special situations, and restricting privileges at one point while releasing forces and individuals at other points.

National Planning Board, *Board Report 1933–1934*
(Federal Emergency Administration of Public Works, 1934)

3
Comprehensive Planning

> Planning, as part of development policy management more generally, is not simply about the technicalities of economic analysis however important these might be. Neither is it simply about ensuring that it is linked to the political process. . . . In addition it has to be overwhelmingly about political leadership and statesmanship.
>
> Editorial, "Planning Has to be About Political Leadership and Statesmanship," *DPMN Bulletin*, April 1993, p. 3

MECHANISM FOR PLANNING

As discussed previously in this book, human societies cannot exist and function without forethought in some form. The remarkable advances in science and technology which are transforming our world have required extensive planning. The products, services, and complex systems integrating hundreds or millions of components into single operating entities, which have resulted from these advances, have not come about by chance. They are the result of a high order of planning. Sophisticated household equipment, the modern automobile, energy, and communication systems are familiar examples. Private enterprise and the military services are incorporating more and more comprehensive planning in their operations as they become more complicated. Planning as presently practiced is the subject of chapter 1.

As noted at the end of the previous chapter, it is at the highest levels of government that we are not planning successfully, with the most serious and potentially devastating consequences for the nation and our democratic society. The critical problems in the United States today noted throughout this book have many underlying and related causes, but they are not being resolved or at least kept from getting worse, because there is little or no comprehensive planning at the legislative levels of government. The absence of such planning by Congress is the primary obstacle to improving current conditions and the prospects for our nation and society in the future. Because the most devastating problems confronting us today are national in their causes and effects, they require directive action or coordination at the federal level of societal governance.

Congress cannot successfully fulfill its managerial as well as representative responsibilities unless it abandons certain prevailing practices which have evolved over the years and prevent effective directive management today. Actions addressing the nation's most serious problems cannot be considered separately as they are now, rather than as part of a societal entity composed of many interrelated elements. The politics of individual, partisan, parochial, and special interests must yield to the broader politics of the nation at large, the general public interest, and the society as a whole. All policies, decisions, plans, and actions must be related analytically to the capabilities, limitations, and needs of the nation as a societal entity; to previous commitments made by Congress and by others; and to activities that have been programmed for the future. There is also the problem of the large size of Congress, the large number and size of its committees and subcommittees, and its procedural and organizational inefficiencies. Above all, the fundamental mechanism for comprehensive planning is missing.

Simulation

Comprehensive planning requires a simulation or depictive representation of the entity being planned. The most basic form of simulation are concepts in our minds that we refer to when we determine how we will conduct our daily affairs or some other purposeful activity. Heads of families and the owners or operators of small businesses have in their minds an internalized picturization of the family unit or the business which they can mentally refer to and judge what is feasible or desirable, and what is beyond their capabilities or is undesirable for other reasons. Working drawings, construction specifications, and cost estimates on paper or a computer disk simulate a proposed structure before it is approved and built. The sounds on a stethoscope and the images produced by various diagnostic instruments represent the physical condition of the patient for the physician and determine what he prescribes. Four operational statements simulate the functioning of a small business sufficiently for elementary planning purposes and can make the difference between success and failure: operating statement, profit-and-loss statement, balance sheet, and record of cash flow. About one-half of private enterprise in the United States consists of small businesses with fewer than fifty employees, and about one-half of these will fail within ten years because of poor planning. In the military services, simulations of warfare range from speculative scenarios and computer programs to mock troop exercises in the field. In peacetime, the military services spend a large part of their time planning what they would do under various hostile situations. With the end of the Cold War between the United States and the Soviet Union, the military services are being called upon for peacekeeping purposes, a new role for them quite different from waging war. In both of these activities simulation of the expected situation is an essential part of the preparatory planning.

Every organization and activity consists of certain components: the people who comprise it, the time available for them to work and produce, and the other resources available. They can be represented separately and as they interrelate by whatever simulation most accurately depicts the functioning of the organism or activity in real life. Together with current conditions and special circumstances outside the organization affecting its operations, its fundamental characteristics as represented in the simulation indicate what can and cannot be accomplished and suggest what actions should be taken. Proposed policies, projects, plans, procedural changes, and alternative actions are introduced into the analytical simulation to test their feasibility and probable consequences for the organization or activity.

Simulations have been employed in the United States more for operational control than for planning purposes. Utility companies use them to monitor and direct an electric power, gas distribution, or water supply system. In a large room designed for the purpose, the geographical disposition of the utility supply system and its components are displayed graphically on the walls, with lights or other indicators recording the condition of different elements and the entire system. When some part fails or the system is disrupted for some other reason, adjustments can usually be made to temporarily bypass the point of failure and restore uninterrupted service. Operational simulations are used by telephone companies to route transcontinental calls across the United States, to reduce delays, avoid overloading some circuits, and to handle as many telephone calls as possible. Railroads with systems covering many states keep track of and schedule rolling stock on displays similar to those used by utility companies, to ensure that railroad cars and locomotives are being used and not sitting idle because of poor operational planning. In times of emergency, when a natural hazard or operational failure has interrupted rail traffic, the simulation of the system is used to determine the best way to restore normal service.

In the military services, visual displays simulating many thousands of square miles in space are the primary instrumentality of military command centers, such as those for North American air defense, aircraft and ship deployment around an aircraft carrier, monitoring the some six thousand objects orbiting the earth, or the Situation Room in the White House where materials needed in making critical decisions are displayed. Computers and data storage are an integral part of the type of simulation we are considering here, but few are formulated entirely within the computer and displayed only on the computer screen. Some larger visual or graphic displays are needed for the final decision makers who do not have time to keep up with the ever-changing details of computer programming, and usually prefer the simplest possible larger scale portrayal of the essential information they must understand and consider.

Members of Congress have an administrative staff to support them in whatever way they choose. Probably at least one-half of staff time and effort are spent on purely political matters: maintaining contact with the electorate, assisting in the solicitation of campaign funds, and servicing the interests and particular concerns of major political supporters. Perhaps one-half of their time may be spent on substantive study relating to proposed legislation, committee or other congressional activities and concerns. Congress also has available to it the supportive offices noted at the end of the last chapter: the Congressional Budget Office, General Accounting Office, Office of Technology Assessment, and the Congressional Research Service of the Library of Congress. Each of these can provide information and analysis concerning a particular concern of a member of Congress or of one of its committees, which is within the supporting office's assignment and competence. Congress can request studies by any federal department or independent agency, if it does not preempt too much time and effort from their prescribed activities.

These existing sources can provide information and analysis concerning specific problems and issues. They do not and cannot provide the simulation required for sound comprehensive planning by Congress, which must incorporate the essential elements of the national political and societal entity which is the object of legislative decision making and planning. It must include basic information concerning the population of the United States, the economy, politics, housing and other physical facilities, transportation and communication, social conditions, legal requirements and constraints, customs and beliefs, and defense and security. The interrelationships between components are calculated and incorporated as part of the simulation, so that the effects of actions taken or proposed for one element on other elements can be determined. It must also include information concerning the past: commitments made years ago which apply today and extend into the future; data which indicate trends; experience which is relevant today; and established customs and beliefs to be taken into account. At least some of the information is projected into the future to extrapolate trends and as part of analyzing what actions are most likely to produce the desired results at some future time.

The simulation is continuously brought up-to-date. This is easily done for information recorded, maintained, and available as a display on the computer screen. Flexible graphical materials permit rapid change of the wall displays that present the essential core of information and analysis all legislators can comprehend personally and discuss in groups. It is this clearly expressed display that is accessible to the public, so that those interested or concerned know the national situation which existed at the time actions were taken by their elected representatives. They can also tell in many instances the extent to which the societal situation as revealed by the simulation was taken into account in legislative decision making.

Implications

Incorporation of a simulation as the key element in planning signifies several fundamental changes in the planning process. In government, it indicates that rational analysis has prevailed over purely emotional, partisan political, special interest, parochial, or selfish concerns as the primary considerations in planning and administrative management. With simulation, the scope of planning shifts toward the governmental and societal unit as a whole, rather than limited to one or several of its components. Longer range plans are more likely to be undertaken, although they are politically riskier than shorter range programs; initial public support for the longer range plan may change to active opposition before it is realized years hence, threatening the re-election of legislators who voted for it. With the analytical information provided by the simulation as a reference, reaching conclusions and making decisions takes more time and effort. But it also discourages superficial consideration of important matters, careless conclusions, and irresponsible decisions. Planning becomes more thoughtful, professional, and intellectually more rigorous. Some legislators may prefer the easier rather than the sounder and more demanding approach. Comprehensive simulation represents the difference between planning that is restricted in scope and planning that is seriously conceived and comprehensively conducted in the general public interest.

The availability and use of a representation depicting the functioning of an organization or activity leads to a more realistic determination of priorities, to comprehensive rather than piecemeal planning. For example, at the congressional level, if the escalating national debt, the rising cost of paying interest on it, and its restrictive effects on other elements of the economy are clearly and persistently portrayed, it is more difficult to forget or ignore the worsening societal situation brought about by continuing to increase the debt. Billions of dollars must be spent during the 1990s to repair, replace, and maintain thousands of roads, bridges, and other physical facilities throughout the country, which were built at about the same time and have deteriorated at about the same rate. If the costs of restoration and the funds available for capital improvement are projected and displayed in the simulation for all to see, it will force consideration of whether desirable but nonessential capital projects can also be funded. Or by clearly revealing the relationship between taxes and financing capital improvements, it will raise the question of alternative funding: more toll roads, toll bridges, and user-financed public facilities. Graphic portrayal of the rapidly changing composition of our population and its relation to social service costs, housing, education, delinquency, and crime will help determine the best allocation of available resources among overwhelming needs and numerous desires. When the capability of the nation—people, time, money, physical plant, and natural resources—is portrayed for all to see and understand, the desire to explore galactic space, police the world, and provide everyone with the good life shown on television may be questioned rather than presumed.

The simulation is for planning purposes. It is not a means of recording, monitoring, and managing operational activities as are several of the examples of simulation noted earlier in this section. Development of a reliable analytical reference for congressional planning purposes is a difficult intellectual task. It must begin simply, with a few elements of the entity; it must be depicted by data readily available and it must be unquestioned accuracy with its primary elements interrelated as to cause and effect. As more elements are added, they are analytically interrelated with the previous material comprising the simulation. It is these interrelationships that are the more difficult to calculate. Some of the elements of the simulation cannot be quantified, but if they are relevant and significant they must be interrelated in some way with other components. The simulation as it exists at any time can be tested by comparing its interactions with the actual behavior of the organization or activity represented. Predictions and assumptions derived from the simulation, concerning what would occur under certain conditions or if certain actions were taken, can be compared with what actually occurs. Extenuating circumstances and events occurring within or outside the organism must be taken into account when determining the accuracy of what the simulation forecast would occur as a consequence of actions taken. This is especially important when the consequences of an action will not be known until some time after the action is taken. Needed adjustments in the simulation revealed by such comparisons are made so that progressively it represents more accurately the organization or activity as it actually functions in the real world.

It will take several years to develop a simulation for congressional reference to its fullest potential, but it can be used while under development to initiate comprehensive planning by legislators. Throughout the process of developing, testing, and using the simulation, the simplest and clearest ways of presenting, evaluating, and analyzing information are adopted. The simulation must be comprehensive not only to the legislators, but to those directing the mass media of communication and many others if it is to be used as a basic reference for comprehensive planning.

Planning Center

The graphical wall display of the simulation summarizes and articulates the state of the nation, displaying its most important elements and their interactions so that they can be understood by most people. Since it should be used by members of Congress and their staffs regularly as an essential reference in connection with legislative activities and actions, the display must be located in the capital building close by their offices. It will occupy considerable wall space in the main room of the planning center. Portions can be reproduced on large computer screens in congressional offices, conference and committee hearing rooms, wherever within the capital and other buildings they are desired or needed for legislative purposes. Or photographs of sections of the complete simulative display can be transported for use elsewhere, or published at page size as a printed document with the time delay required for reproduction in this form.

Background information and analysis maintained in the simulation computers can be transmitted immediately within the capital, and by national, international, and intercontinental computer networks to any place in the world. Since confidential information is not disclosed in the simulation used regularly by Congress and available to the public and the mass media, there should be few if any limitations on its dissemination. Its purposes of analytical elucidation and reference promoting legislative reality are advanced by widespread distribution and informed reaction, and its use by individuals and organizations in connection with their own planning and actions. Everyone benefits by public disclosure and discussion of the simulation, except those legislators who refuse to address the serious problems confronting the nation in terms of its real condition.

The simulation, use of computers, communications to gather information, and other support systems constitute the Congressional Planning Center. Since the factual information needed for comprehensive planning is practically the same for both houses of Congress, a single simulation of the national condition should serve both senators and representatives. They may reach different conclusions and take different actions, but they are concerned with the same national entity. If a single simulation is used, the time, trouble, and cost of duplication are avoided, and different ways of gathering the same background data need not be statistically reconciled. More important, by using the same analytical reference, cohesive effort by both houses of Congress is encouraged. Since it is a factual reference and not a political statement, it would make sense for the president and the governors of states to employ the same simulation employed by their legislative bodies. But this is unlikely because of past disagreements between the executive and legislative branches of government concerning their respective form and functioning. Employment of the same simulation would not, in fact, compromise the differences between the two branches intended by the Constitution.

It is clear that what is proposed here is difficult to achieve. It challenges present predilections of legislators to ignore or repeatedly postpone acting on critical problems confronting the nation, to proceed piecemeal when actions are taken, to place special interests and self-interests above public needs, and personal political survival above all else. It requires our elected representatives to act differently than they do now, in ways they do not prefer. It asks them to lead the nation in directions that conditions and circumstances require rather than as emotional reaction and transitory public opinion dictate.

If indeed this is the situation, how can changes be made and better methods of planning introduced? The main impetus for improvement will come from societal developments that threaten political stability if they are not resolved or at least some actions taken toward their resolution. Also, the operational systems of our nation and society require continuous planning. Failure to plan comprehensively and manage more effectively will in time result in political crises and operational chaos which cannot be tolerated.

> Welfare governments have to have knowledge, foresight, well-developed methodologies, and means of insuring that the general interest shall resist the encroachments of special ones. They have, in other words, to plan. . . .
>
> To accept from those who define the general aspirations, their definition of what ought to be, to make this definition precise and practical, to show how much of it is feasible and how that much can be attained. . . .
>
> [The Planning Center] brings hopes into focus and promises into possibility, a protector of reason among competing imaginative conceptions, a reducer of vague expectations to measured charts, tables, and maps. . . .
>
> How does it comport with representative governments? It is, in fact, the only agency of government—whose *only* purpose is to discover and implement the public interest. And since representative institutions are founded on the principle that sovereignty resides in the people, it is profoundly necessary for democracy. . . .

Otherwise the scene is abandoned to a contest between conflicting private and local interests—each seeking its own advantage.[1]

RESEARCH

Despite growing recognition of its vital role in human affairs, little research has been conducted in planning as a distinct subject and universal process with its own theory, principles, and fundamental characteristics.

There are few descriptions of successful planning. Such as the artificial harbor and landing of troops in Normandy during World War II, development of the fission and fusion nuclear weapons, the space shuttle and missions in outer space; designing and manufacturing a large commercial aircraft, an ocean-going vessel, an electronic computer, or a new pharmaceutical product. Also unrecorded is the planning of our organizational and behavioral achievements, which have been far fewer than the physical objects and facilities we have produced: for example, social security and computerized national mail-order systems, air and surface traffic control, worldwide eradication of smallpox, and religious administration.

There are reports, articles, general and specific descriptions of many developments, but few explanations of the process of planning that made them possible. In some cases it is because the information is classified secret for national security or "company confidential" for commercial protection. Most often it is because those involved in planning regard the completed project as sufficient indication in itself of the forethought it required, forgetting that much is to be learned from explaining the ups and downs of the directive process which guided its achievement. Also, the planners have turned to different activities or taken new jobs, with little incentive to take the time to write up their experience on the previous project. A record of this experience should be part of the completion of every major project and its formal termination. Favorable circumstances, fortuitous events, support by certain individuals or organizations, or random chance may have contributed significantly to success, but deliberate planning is always an integral and necessary part of the purposeful process.

An accumulation of descriptive explanations of successful planning would provide an important background for research: identifying successful and unsuccessful procedures, suggesting or confirming theoretical formulations, and establishing general principles with wide application. The experience of planning and achieving some form of universal health insurance in the United States in the mid-1990s is an example of a large, complex, and significant endeavor which should maintain a record of its successes and failures in planning as an addition to a repository of planning experience.

Simulation

Simulation is certainly one of the techniques of planning that should be the subject of continuous research. "Representations of the entirety" take many forms. Small-scale hydrodynamic models of bodies of water simulate for ecological study or the design of shore installations the waves, currents, and turbulence created by tides, weather conditions, and earth tremors. Flight simulators are used to train and test aircraft pilots, huge centrifuges to simulate the G-forces encountered in air combat and weightlessness when orbiting the earth in near outer space. Wind tunnels generate aerodynamic forces to test the design of aircraft and missiles. Mathematical models represent systems whose elements can be expressed in numbers or other quantification. And works of art or literature signify the state of being or situation which they create and treat imaginatively.

The simulation of the state of the nation advocated earlier in this chapter as the primary reference for congressional decision making would itself employ only few forms of representation. The background information derived from many sources which it uses would involve many forms of simulation. As time passes, better ways will be found of expressing and measuring the primary components of the national simulation and their interaction, but its current form can always serve to improve legislative decision making.

Some vital considerations in real life and their simulation for planning purposes cannot be enumerated and compared with elements that are expressed in numbers. These include political factors, most cultural and religious customs and beliefs, legal considerations, many of the attitudes and actions of individuals and organizations, and their emotional reactions and resistance. Any one of these can be more important in the simulation and planning than "hard" facts and figures.

One way of incorporating elements that cannot be quantified is to elicit the opinions of people knowledgeable concerning the matter at hand, as an integral part of the analytical formulation. The Delphi technique of opinion survey is structured to obtain the individual and collective judgments of a small group of experts by a process of questioning, response, and "cross-impact" analysis of replies. It can be used, for example, to estimate when an important scientific advance is likely to be attained, and what must happen before it can occur. The collective judgment of a group of politically astute people may be the best way of deciding if and when an event that is an essential element of a simulation will take place. Scientific sample surveys are available and widely used to enumerate general attitudes and opinions within statistical margins of error. Careful formulation of the questions asked is necessary to avoid built-in bias, and the categorization of replies must meet the requirements of statistical accuracy. Individual judgments and group consensus obtained in these ways can be incorporated in mathematical and statistical formulations when they are necessary to complete an analysis of cause and effect. Sometimes an item in the analysis can only be expressed as between a high and a low value. If the results of the analysis using each extreme do not differ significantly, the indefinite item is not significant in reaching a conclusion.

Are there better ways of integrating the quantifiable and the nonquantifiable, the scientific and nonscientific, rational and irrational, predictable and unpredictable? Since most decisions involve both, this is an important subject for further research in planning.

Market Mechanisms

Market mechanisms are a fact of human activity and economic life in both democratic and autocratic societies. A feature of democracy is providing as much unregulated economic activity as is consistent with the needs, purposes, and survival of the society. Certain functions must be performed or at least directed by government: national political, monetary, banking, tax, and legal systems; basic police protection; and national defense. Others by their nature do not follow supply and demand.

> In health care today, fundamental principles of the marketplace do not apply. Prices are not determined by supply and demand or by competition among producers. Comparison shopping is impossible. Greater productivity does not lower costs. . . . Economists agree that the health-care industry can never work entirely according to the rules

> of the marketplace. [They] also agree that medicine does not have to stray as far outside the marketplace as it does now.[2]

Ideally, the primary elements of the national analytical simulation and their interconnections will reflect that

> combination of freedom for private enterprise and intervention by government in . . . market mechanisms [which] favors: the economic health of the [nation] at different stages of its development; its functioning in the collective best interest of its inhabitants; and the maintenance of as much freedom of choice by the individual and by non-governmental organizations as is consistent with these objectives.[3]

Socioeconomic Indicators

The physical components of the nation can be counted accurately enough to support conclusions and actions with respect to them. The socioeconomic state of the nation, which represents the living conditions and contentment of its population, is difficult to determine. The economic status of most people is known from the information gathered by business for marketing and credit purposes and by government for tax and regulatory purposes. People's satisfaction with living conditions involves much more. For example, the size of the dwelling unit and work space, their character and condition, determine in part their livability and acceptability. But what is substandard for one person or group of people may not be for another ethnic population and culture. Health statistics illuminate only one important aspect of the quality of life, and accurate census data concerning the disadvantaged, underclass, the homeless, and some immigrant groups are lacking.

Personal contentment with living conditions and satisfying relationships with people are probably the most important indicators of the socioeconomic situation of each person, but they are also the most difficult to measure individually and to correlate. Reliable opinion surveys are not only too expensive for regular use, but even with thoroughly structured interviews they cannot measure the combination of factors that determine socioeconomic contentment. Research is needed to develop a more reliable and practical method of determining individual and collective socioeconomic satisfaction. This important part of the national simulation can be observed over time as an indicator of societal progress, and as a basis for evaluating the effects of existing and proposed policies and plans. It might also reveal increasing social tensions that could lead to civil disturbances. Or research may disclose that there are no feasible ways at the present time to do more than impute socioeconomic satisfaction very generally from an assortment of related factors. Efforts are being made.

> "The Index of Social Health" [by the Fordham University Institute for Innovation in Social Policy] attempts to monitor the well-being of American society by examining statistics from reports by the Census Bureau on 16 major social problems, including teen-age suicide, unemployment, drug abuse, the high-school dropout rate, and the lack of affordable housing. Aided by a computer model, the researchers use the statistics from the 16 categories to reach a simple figure between 0 and 100, which they call the index of social health.[4]

Cost-Benefit Analysis

People constantly consider the pros and cons of their actions and intentions. Our financial accounting system compares what can be expressed in monetary units. Statistical systems compare quantities expressed in the same or equivalent terms. Largely because of an increasing awareness and concern with the environment, efforts are being made to identify and measure most of the direct and indirect costs and benefits of whatever nature that relate to an existing or proposed project, activity, or policy.

The great advances in knowledge during the past several centuries reveal that all things, microscopic and macroscopic, are interrelated. Theoretically, every project or activity involves an infinity of interactions. In a simulation of the nation some of these are between primary elements, such as economics and housing, or education and employment. Others occur within an element. Under housing, for example, there are the type, size, condition, cost, utility connections, and sanitary facilities of dwelling units; the mortgage commitment; and insurance coverage. There is a maze of interconnections between such classifications, but only a few are needed for planning purposes. As the number of elements to be considered and the number of factors in each element increases, the grand total increases exponentially. Since successful planning requires analysis of only a small fraction of existing interrelationships, cost-benefit calculations can be incorporated at reasonable cost and useful accuracy.

Risk Analysis

Humans have faced environmental hazards throughout their evolutionary development. Survival required protection against extreme heat and cold, predators, and natural hazards; obtaining food and water; and successful reproduction. Meeting these requirements and surviving the risks involved depended on individual effort, a supportive family, and a societal group functioning cooperatively and helping those of its members in need.

In the past several hundred years of rapid scientific and technological development, new hazards have joined those of socioeconomic survival: hazards associated with modern transportation and modern workplaces, environmental contamination, and the global effects of human activities on the chemical composition of the upper atmosphere. At the same time, we expect or want protection against more and more risks. It is inevitable that people seek as much protection from hazards and as much compensation for losses and injury as possible. If not from prepaid insurance, people believe relief should be provided by the government from general taxes, as a humane response and as a way of restoring economically productive activity in a devastated area.

For the most part, the public is unaware of the great differences in statistical risk associated with different hazards, their relation to the general death rate from disease as a measure of comparative significance, and the cost of other societal consequences of reducing the risk by human action. No society has the resources to minimize all hazards. A choice is made, explicitly or implicitly, between different dangers and the extent of protection that is applied to each. Prevention has to do with rules and regulations. For example, reducing the potential hazards involved in constructing and operating buildings and other physical facilities, health standards decreasing the risks of food poisoning and infectious disease, or rules of the road reducing traffic accidents and injury. Protection deals with the consequences of disastrous events: levees to protect against floods, underground tornado shelters, seat belts and air bags, paramedics to treat injury, and insurance to pay for various losses.

People's reaction to risks relates to the extent they are taken voluntarily. We accept the risks involved when we elect to drive a car, fly in an airplane, or use equipment that is potentially dangerous. We are less likely to tolerate hazards that are imposed on us, such as environmental hazards which someone else creates, or natural disasters which no one can control or affect. We are prone to ask government to compensate us for the damage caused by the acts of others and by nature. Or we rely on insurance, personal choices concerning how and where we live, and other ways of compensating for the risks we accept. Or we ignore them.

Risk analysis seeks to determine and to disclose the relative danger for the individual and the population as a whole of various hazards, the costs of reducing or not reducing the risk, and the consequences for society of these considerations. In democracies, the body politic ultimately decides what its elected representatives must do with respect to risks. If sufficiently informed, the public is more likely to make a rational decision. If not, public reaction to risks is irrational rather than thoughtful, relying on insufficient or erroneous information, emotional reaction, or depending on which hazards have recently dominated the news. Without public expression, the treatment of risks is by people's choices in the commercial marketplace of insurance and in the political arena of legislative action.

Risks are part of every element in a national simulation, because they are involved in every aspect of human life. Collectively they might constitute an element in themselves, if methods of calculating and integrating a large number and variety of risks are developed. Large costs are involved. And there is always the underlying question of the desirability and the capability of everyone in the country paying for everybody else's recovery from disastrous events.

PROFESSIONAL EDUCATION AND OCCUPATION

Until shortly after the turn of the century, planning in the United States was not identified and taught as a separate subject. It was incorporated as an essential aspect of most fields of knowledge. Planning was first identified specifically as part of graduate education in landscape architecture, architecture, and engineering, and to a lesser extent in public and business administration. Its function in architecture and engineering was so clear and unmistakable that it led to its specific recognition. When working drawings, construction specifications, and cost estimates are required for all architectural and engineering projects—simulating the completed structure—there can be little doubt that planning is of the essence. It is also essential in public and business administration, but less apparent because there is no requirement for the detailed simulative documents, needed in architecture and engineering, to secure local governmental approval of the proposed project, construction loans from a bank or investment group, and advance commitments to occupy space in the structure or to make use of the physical facility before it is finished. A business plan, however, can exist in the head or files of the chief executive awaiting implementation and public announcement. A governmental plan may remain in the minds of legislators until it is politically feasible to proceed. Legislators would prefer never committing themselves publicly and irrevocably to longer range plans which may be unpopular with the electorate at re-election time.

> The first use of the word planning in an educational program was in city planning. The first formal university training in city planning was not introduced until 1909, and then only in a few separate courses given to students of landscape architecture. Training in architecture, landscape architecture, and engineering was then seen as adequate for the planning tasks. Not until 1923 was city planning accepted as a graduate specialization, and then only in one department in one university (Harvard).[5]

There are now more than 100 graduate departments of urban and regional planning associated with schools of architecture, landscape architecture, civil engineering, geography, environmental studies, political science, government, public administration, and social work. Master's degrees predominate in these programs, but at least a dozen departments award Ph.D. degrees. Planning has also been an educational emphasis in schools of public and business administration, and in war colleges and special educational programs devoted to military operations and planning.

However, at present, none of these programs teaches or conducts related research in comprehensive planning as a fundamental process involved in all human activities, in one way or another, to a greater or lesser extent. This requires incorporating subject matter not now covered in existing curricula.

For example, effective planning cannot be conducted without at least minimum information concerning the organization or activity involved. It must have the necessary content and reliability. It must be available or procurable. It must be analyzed and used in planning. But this basic requirement of successful planning is not included in existing educational programs in urban and regional planning. None of them treat electromagnetic "remote sensing", although it provides more information for more purposes than the U.S. Census or any other means of obtaining information. Nor is simulation—described briefly in chapter 3 on pages 120 and 121—covered as a crucial element in all planning, whether by civil government, business, or the military services.

The content of professional education often consists of what each instructor prefers to teach, rather than the body of knowledge that provides the best foundation for future practice and research. When comprehensive planning is generally recognized as essential for the successful conduct of human affairs, it will be taught as a distinct intellectual discipline involving elements and aspects not now included or inadequately covered in the several forms of partial education now available.

Diversity is found not only in the association of planning with different academic fields, but also in the variety of positions in government, business, and the military services which include the word planning in their titles. They are found at all levels of management, from high-ranking executives to low-level supervisors and team leaders. Corporate planning has been established as a staff position in the top management of large corporations. Directors of planning are part of the executive administration of many public organizations. Planning positions have to do with all kinds of subjects and activities: policies, finance, resource allocation, budgets, marketing, transportation, land use, production, recreation, personnel, public relations. The list is almost endless. Some positions involve short-range tactical or operational plans, others long-range strategic objectives. Staff planners conduct planning analysis for line executives. Operating managers apply planning to the activities within their organizational jurisdiction or directive authority, often with a planning assistant or staff of their own to provide background analysis.[6]

There are two professional planning associations with local chapters in the United States. Most of the twenty-seven thousand members of the American Planning Association—seven thousand of whom have qualified for its American Institute of Certified Planners—work for civil governments and private consulting firms which conduct studies for many of them under contract. They are concerned with the use of land in municipalities, counties, and states. They prepare master plans and regulations relating to the use and development of land, for consideration or adoption by their respective legislatures which make the final decisions. The primary interest and occupational activities of most members are expressed by incorporating the word "planning" in the title of the position or its organizational description.

The eight thousand or so members of the International Society for Planning and Strategic Management are engaged in planning in private enterprise. They are involved in one of the many different applications of planning in business: corporate planning, budgeting, executive management, administration, finance, marketing, or research and analysis. The word planning may not be incorporated in the title of the position, but it is part of the job description.

The association of planning with different academic concentrations and the diversity of its operational applications exemplify the uniqueness and universality of the process. It could not have so many associations and applications were it not in itself a distinct field of knowledge and employment. Like mathematics, it is an intellectual discipline which is part of or operates in almost every area of inquiry and endeavor. It will be taught as a distinct theoretical and applied field of knowledge. Development of a general theory and principles of planning is under way. People will be educated and trained to perform the functions proposed in this book. The place for planning as a substantive and professional capability in human affairs is assured, since it is a determinative part of the vital activities of society.

REFERENCES

1. Rexford G. Tugwell, *The Place of Planning in Society*, Technical Paper 7, Puerto Rico Planning Board, 1954, p. 38.

2. David E. Rosenbaum, "America's Economic Outlaw: The U.S. Health Care System," *The New York Times*, 26 October 1993, p. zA1.

3. Melville C. Branch, "Critical Unresolved Problems of Urban Planning Analysis," *Journal of the American Institute of Planners*, January 1978, p. 50.

4. "Researchers Say U.S. Social Well-Being Is 'Awful'," *The New York Times*, 18 October 1993, p. A12z.

5. Harvey S. Perloff, *Education for Planning: City, State, & Regional* (Baltimore: Johns Hopkins, 1957), p. 11.

6. Melville C. Branch, *Planning: Universal Process* (New York: Praeger, 1990), pp. 128–133.

Rather than let the press fix the news priorities and batter the president . . . the White House intended to set not only the political agenda for Congress but also the television agenda for the networks.

"We wanted to control what people saw to the extent we could . . . to shape it and not let television shape it. . . . You had to figure out how to [control] it on your own. I mean, large aspects, the public aspects, of government have become staged, television-staged, and there is a real question who is going to control the stage. Is it going to be the networks or the people who work for the candidate or for the president."

That's what it comes down to—we are marketing. . . . We are trying to mold public opinion by marketing strategies. That's what communications is all about . . . trying to close a sale or make a sale, and that's what I'm doing with public opinion: creating events that convey a message. Many of our little playlets, or presidential events, have a relationship to the advertising business."

David Gergen, William Henkel
quoted in Hedrik Smith, *The Power Game*
(Random House, 1988)

4

Role of the Mass Media

I spoke with a worker [in Thailand] . . . who told me that she lived with her father-in-law and two sons, aged four months and three years, in a bamboo hut with a tin roof. The hut was about twelve feet square, she said, and had no partitions. The only appliance was a television set. . . . Another sewing machine operator, told me that she lives with her parents and a brother and sister in a one-room shack with a tin roof and a mud floor. It had electricity and a television set, but no plumbing.

James Lardner, "Annals of Business: The Sweater Trade–1," *New Yorker*, 11 January 1988

Rupert Murdock is close to creating the first truly global television empire . . . the potential of reaching two-thirds of the world's population. Star's five satellite channels can be seen in 38 nations in Asia and the Middle East. . . . MTV is a cultural phenomenon, altering the musical tastes and buying habits of tens of millions of middle-class Asian teenagers. . . . Millions of Asian adults now get their news from BBC World Service Television. . . . Mr. Murdock has said through spokesmen that he has no intention of interfering in the political affairs of the nations that receive Star TV.

Philip Shenon, "Star TV Extends Murdock's Reach," *The New York Times*, 25 August 1993

FUNDAMENTAL REQUIREMENTS

Because communication is the backbone and nerve cord of the societal body, the primary requirement for the mass media is to provide a communication system that enables the nation to function and to survive. It is so vital that in modern warfare communication centers are primary targets. If the system is knocked out defensive weapons do not operate effectively, military command is disrupted, and public morale is impaired because people have difficulty contacting one another. This chapter discusses the major nontechnical considerations in such a system in a democratic society.

A basic question is whether those who want or need to interact must know or must learn a common national language which is the primary and official spoken and written means of communicating. Or whether a society can and should provide "equal communication" in different languages. If so, in how many languages, how selected? Even if in the future automatic and immediate computer translation of any language into any other is possible, the inevitable differences remain of nuance and exact meaning and the need for a standard and official reference. Mass communication must not only be intelligible to the great majority of the populace, it must also be factually accurate. Granted there can be differences of opinion concerning what is accurate, 99% of factual information does not involve subtle questions of substantive meaning, but whether it was accurately collected and compiled. Inadvertent or deliberate dissemination of inaccurate information can mislead the electorate and misdirect its activities, with serious if not fatal consequences in a democracy. The mass media must contribute constructively to society. Inducements to lawlessness, violence, deliberate disruption, or revolutionary action by force cannot be tolerated in a society that wishes to remain democratic. Ownership of many television and radio stations, telecomputer systems, and newspapers enables an individual or organization to influence people disproportionately among the diverse voices essential in a free society. Carried to an extreme, this can threaten democratic institutions.

At the same time, the mass media must be able to act as both critic and advocate for the society, its institutions, and its actions. Including the postal service and telephone systems as mass media of communication, there is no other way in a democracy of calling attention to serious problems that are being ignored, revealing misbehavior and corruption, disclosing inefficiency and mismanagement, excesses and inequalities, or malfeasance at the highest levels of government and private enterprise. As an objective observer of society, its operation, and its governance, the mass media are obligated to raise serious questions concerning all sectors of society. Although criticism and faultfinding are considered more newsworthy than compliments and commendation, the mass media are equally responsible for calling attention to laudable actions and accomplishments. They must be able to conduct investigative reporting to fulfill both these functions without fear of retribution.

Civil government, private enterprise, the military services, and all other institutions and activities in a democratic society are subject to the watchdog eye and ear of the mass media. This function of evaluation, disclosure, and reporting bears with it the responsibility of acting constructively, accurately, and in the general public interest putting aside biases at least temporarily when reporting as the "fourth estate". This requires deliberate attention and effort by news and investigative reporters, few of whom have had experience in the human affairs they report and evaluate. As their title indicates, reporters are commentators rather than doers in an operational sense. In their role as societal appraisers, they must balance their ingrained desire to include as much "news" as possible in their reports, with the need to incorporate less "newsworthy" aspects when they are more truly descriptive or evaluative of the subject under consideration.

The mass media must not become such a dogmatic power in themselves that they become, in fact, the governing force in society. The fundamental requirements for a national communication system to operate in the general public interest can never be ignored or taken for granted in a democracy.

Acknowledging Reality

Almost everyone connected with the mass media in the United States regards any questioning of the way their particular activity is conducted as threatening their freedom of speech guaranteed in the first amendment of the U.S. Constitution. This has become for those in the communication business an automatic reaction and an immediate unqualified defense of existing procedures, more than a thoughtful response and justification.

> I think the minimum of what we should be doing as writers is talking about [violence on TV]. But when I try to get a conversation started with other writers, I hear the argument that just talking about it is putting yourself in the hands of censors.[1]

If carried to its logical extreme, no questioning of the existing operations or content of mass communications, nor any suggestions involving change in present practices, is to be seriously considered. By refusing to treat certain subjects, those who control the media and those who pay for broadcast time and communication in print can reduce public discussion of the function and operation of mass communications. Legislators and others whose careers depend on television are reluctant to express any criticism or even constructive suggestion. Discussion within the Federal Communications Commission is not reported to the public at large.

The mass media are so central to societal life that discussion of their role and performance should be encouraged rather than dismissed under the pretext that it does not matter. They are the primary source of news and information. They shape public attitudes in general and the specific responses of people to particular situations and events. The mass media can generate public opinion which forces action by government and by private enterprise. They determine more than anything else who is elected and to a large extent who is confirmed for the highest decision-making positions in government. Failure to engage in open debate can no longer be explained by the unrealistic claim that television and radio provide only innocuous entertainment, and that the print media are only reportive without influencing public opinion and choice.

Rather than attempting to cover the mass media separately, this chapter concentrates on television and telecomputing screens as the predominant focal points of communication in the future. They present and display the information to the viewer.

What should be considered and what occurs with regard to telecomputing will apply sooner or later to the other means of mass communication.

Ownership

The owners of television and radio stations and interactive telecomputer systems have the greatest control over these most important means of mass communication. Subject to minimum requirements by the Federal Communications Commission (FCC), and depending on what those who pay for TV exposure require, what is broadcast is the owner's decision whether he makes it personally or delegates it to someone else.

> Networks exercise absolute veto power over the scripts of their TV writers, with any element, including the entire story, subject to rejection on almost any basis at all. Feature film scripts . . . are written to the taste of the producer, who writes the checks and who has veto power on any issue, including aesthetics, conscience, taste, or anything else.[2]

Advertisers foot the bill, TV disseminates their message. Both owners and advertisers maintain that viewer response measured by audience ratings is the only justifiable method of program selection and content.

> If the public wants good TV programming, then it should support the good shows that come on. . . . The public enthusiasm for violent films is an endorsement of them. It's a consumer society. The studio heads are just business people.[3]

Owners and advertisers do not accept research that indicates that television can create viewer acceptance and viewer demand, particularly among children and adolescents. They do not concur publicly that the choice of which of the multitude of news items available to broadcast, and which to omit, influences viewer reactions. Nor that the frequent repetition of a particular event on television, especially an emotionally disturbing photographic view, can intensify viewers' reactions to the event and fix it firmly in their minds and memories. They do not agree that every

TV program we view affects our attitudes in some way, a little or a lot as the case may be. Some owners deliberately challenge any boundaries of acceptable language and content in broadcasting, maintaining that there are no extremes of violent, obscene, and irresponsible language and expression that justify restrictions and penalties.

> Even the bigger fines [by the FCC] represent little more than pocket change for large broadcasters and have done little to slow the number of imitators. A number of conservative organizations have petitioned the FCC to hit the broadcaster where it really hurts—its ability to buy stations.[4]

There is no publicly expressed opinion among owners whether there should be any limit to the number of TV and radio stations and telecomputer systems a single individual or organization can own or control. In the final analysis, it appears that self-interest—measured by profits and personal or organizational power—determines what private entrepreneurs consider is best for society. TV's impact on people and its role in society deserve less self-centered, more honest, and more realistic consideration.

Violent Content

The increasing violence shown on television as entertainment is only part of the reality that is disregarded or even denied by its perpetrators. This unmistakable trend is confirmed not only by actual counts of violent episodes, but by the testimony of no less a person than the attorney general of the United States before a congressional committee that violence has been "ground into us, day in and day out." The increase in violence has been accompanied by an increase in the portrayal of deliberate cruelty and disregard for law and morality. Compassion, consideration for others, unselfishness, good citizenship, even courtesy are rarely seen on the TV screen. As if this were not enough to deepen concern, there is an increasing display of guns, rapid-fire weapons, and shooting which at times is a continuous rain of bullets for minutes on end. Scenes of sexual intercourse, rape, and perversions multiply. All this in the name of entertainment for American audiences and for foreign viewers receiving the programs by satellite.

Animated cartoons for children—broadcast in the early morning hours to fulfill the FCC requirement for a minimum number of televised programs for the young—are filled with aggressive actions, deadly weapons, violence, and abnormaliteis of various kinds. Incorporation of destructive objects and hostile behavior in the events and activities depicted in make-believe telescenarios affects the crucial process of learning to differentiate between fact and fiction which all children experience. Many of the video games which young people love to play involve warfare, armed conflict, fierce and hostile competition, and cruelty. One such video in the early 1990s included so many decapitations that protest by parents forced voluntary withdrawal. The societally important question is why was it produced and made available for widespread viewing in the first place? Few animated cartoons and video games deal with personally and societally constructive attitudes and actions.

Unrestrained Competition

Underlying these trends are the built-in dynamics of unrestrained competition noted in chapter 2. The creators and purveyors of television programs and presentations battle among themselves for the higher audience ratings that bring increased advertising and other promotional revenues, and greater profits. Each does whatever it takes to entice, excite, titillate, or otherwise attract and hold a larger market share of the finite number of TV viewers. This has produced the situation noted in the previous paragraph. Those who determine what will be broadcast have promoted or acquiesced in the escalation of more and more violent, cruel, and prurient content. And those who work for them and are otherwise employed in television production are caught up in the syndrome of attracting more viewers by catering to primitive human characteristics which civilization seeks to sublimate. The focus is on instincts, fears, passions, or superstitious beliefs rather than on the thoughtful reactions, constructive actions, and more civilized behavior which stabilize a society and enhance its prospects. Producers, directors, and scriptwriters favor more and more emotionally stimulating and addictive material. Cameramen seek the most dramatic heartrending, violent, or penetrating shots in depicting sexual intercourse on the screen. Some news announcers dress up and act up to dramatize straightforward presentation of the news.

There is nothing innately wrong or harmful in basic human emotions and the residual primitive drives and immature characteristics we all share. It is when they are exercised with less and less restraint that they become personally hurtful and societally disruptive, damaging, or destructive. At the present time, in 1994, there are no stated limitations. Station owners, network officials, program producers, and directors see no reason to change as long as someone will pay for and enough people will watch the program. Most of those who control television broadcasting consider this an appropriate criterion of proper performance, because it is based on "facts and figures" derived from real life. Even were a majority of the controlling group to favor change, collective action is prevented because there is always some member who disagrees and is willing to act independently and make the most of any competitive advantage. There is an adage that no organization can police itself because there is always the dissenting member who will prevent or emasculate corrections or disciplinary action.

> You can't count on the TV industry to examine itself. You can count on it to ignore, redirect, or smoke-screen the issue when it comes to their own industry.[5]

Although more people, especially wives and mothers, are beginning to complain about violence and other objectionable content on television, the viewing audience has not expressed any overall reactions forcing changes in program content. A number of questions remain unanswered. Are people in the United States satisfied with the TV programs and content presented? Is there a way they can express their judgment and desires concerning the medium? Do audience ratings measure satisfaction as well as program choice? Are viewers aware of the impacts of TV on them and on society? Are enough alternatives shown for most viewers to compare what is currently presented with what could be made available? Conclusive answers to these questions have not been obtained. If changes are called for, they will be difficult to effect because of the power of television interests and their insistence that present practices should not be questioned. Many people are reluctant or unwilling to criticize or suggest changes because they depend in some way on TV exposure. Legislators fear losing TV coverage and businesses do not want to disturb the advertising goose that lays golden eggs.

Operational Considerations

There are operational considerations concerning TV that most people are not aware of or do not have occasion to think about. With regard to society as a whole, television can panic a country and conceivably many countries if one or more preeminent TV stations decided to do so or inadvertently triggered such a reaction. Years ago, the fictional program titled "Invasion from Mars", written and directed by Orson Welles, panicked thousands of radio listeners in New York City and nearby New Jersey, despite an announcement at the beginning of the broadcast that it was fiction, not fact. Several years ago the highly respected journal *Science* reported the following:

> Schools will be closing, factories will be shutting down, and families will be fleeing to safer ground. Why? Because that's the day [an] iconoclast scientist . . . has predicted a killer earthquake will strike. . . . Midwesterners didn't get much help from the media in dealing with the unsettling prediction.[6]

A hypothetical or unfounded announcement can cause thousands of people to act in panic or false expectation. We are still close enough to our primitive origins to be susceptible to group frenzy when some happening or combination of events causes us to act in most unusual and peculiar ways.

> Officials are still trying to explain the hysteria. Racial violence had been little known. . . . It seems a combination of boredom, frustration, fear, anger, and ghoulish television-fed fantasy had slowly built to breaking-point. . . . When the police came and then television crews, rumor became fact and the place snapped.[7]

As the main means of communication, television is obligated not to cause panic, chaotic confusion, or needless widespread emotional stress and strain. There is probably an unspoken agreement to this effect among those who control the mass media. But there is no such written prohibition available for public review, nor any declaration of responsibility for the accuracy of the information broadcast, including unsubstantiated allegations and unfounded rumors which can irrevocably damage or destroy individual and organizational reputations and prospects.

The fifteen- or thirty-second pronouncements paid for by one of the political parties, or their supporters, or someone else wishing to make a political statement are broadcast repeatedly at election time to drive home what are often either false allegations or deliberately misleading content. Certainly, rigged and blatantly false advertising, as occurred in two widely publicized instances involving automobiles, should not only be prohibited but the advertiser should be fined and denied access to television for a period of time. And if a TV station knowingly broadcasts false information, it should be required to cease all broadcasting for a penalty period. Other deception should also be disallowed and penalized whenever it occurs, such as "infomercials" promoting a product or service under the guise of entertainment, news items cleverly constructed to incorporate an advertisement, or the inclusion in entertainment programs of dialogue or highly visible "props" serving as an advertisement. If subliminal images can be broadcast and absorbed unconsciously by viewers, they should be prohibited to prevent all sorts of unwitting inducement.

Many programs filled with violence and cruelty are broadcast nowadays without even a specious redeeming reason or retributive consequence. Grossly indecent language is aired as a deliberate challenge to societally accepted limitations and existing regulatory restrictions. Ways of committing crimes that cannot be detected are explained or inadvertently disclosed on news and other TV programs. Crimes which have been covered include arson, cheating at gambling, illegal use of payphones, construction of homemade guns, and making illegal explosives from readily available materials. Such explanations are an open invitation to TV viewers inclined to crime and children eager to experiment. Events or conditions with high emotional content are broadcast repeatedly to attract viewers, regardless of consequences. They can create attitudes, heighten latent passions, inure people to violence, or motivate them to war. None of these transgressions would be allowed on a responsibly regulated national information system. And monitors would be alert to the never-ending attempts to violate established limitations to gain competitive advantage or to attain a societally undesirable objective.

Technical manipulation of photographic and sound recordings can change them to the point of falsification. Live audience response can be enhanced or diminished from what actually occurred, or it can be eliminated entirely giving the impression that the event was received with dead silence. Studio audiences can be selected and coached in advance to react as desired by the producers of the TV program. Photographic images can be undetectibly altered to emphasize or de-emphasize portions of a picture, to create an image very different than the original. Voices are substituted one for another—so-called "lip-synching"—without indicating that this has been done. Voices and sounds can be simulated electronically. Technical manipulation has reached the point that it can completely alter the actual recorded image and content of an event, without the viewer being aware that this has been done. Information could be changed to such an extent that viewers would be reacting and acting in response to an illusion created and disseminated by TV. This capacity to create illusions on television is being enhanced by advances in the techniques of "virtual reality", which intensify the viewer's sense that he is actually within the three-dimensional space depicted on the two-dimensional TV screen.

Integrated and Interactive Information

At the present time, most of us watch television, listen to the radio, talk on the telephone, read the newspaper, receive postal mail, and use a personal computer at different times and at different locations in the home or office. They are separate means of communication. There are, of course, interrelationships among them. Radio and television broadcast schedules that are printed in newspapers. Video cassettes of some television programs can be ordered by telephone. One of every four telephone calls nowadays is to send a written, printed, or graphical message by facsimile. The battery-energized radio and the telephone are the instruments of communication and last resort in emergencies when electric power has been cut off. News broadcasts on television and radio are often based on coverage by newspaper reporters or on material originally published in professional, scientific, or other journals. Certain basic electronic components are part of television sets, radios, telephones, and computers. Even the newspaper, bought or delivered one step removed from its printing, was probably typeset electronically.

Such interrelationships among the primary means of mass communication have been developing for some time, but they are few and far between compared with what is now under way and projected for the future. Television, radio, telephone, written and printed word on paper, movies, and the computer will be integrated into a single instrument of multiple communication and interaction at one location in the home and one in the workplace. Today, those of us with telephones can respond immediately or "talk back" to the person with whom we are connected electronically. Those who have personal computers can do this with others connected in an electronic network. And "ham operators" can converse with those who have radio receiver-transmitters with sufficient power anywhere in the world. With the telecomputer to come, we will be able to interact in many more ways. We can receive personal communications and mail from far and wide on the screen. It will display the news, a journal or book of our choice, or read aloud the information for the blind and those with severely impaired eyesight. Many materials and programs will be available in different languages. We will be able to call up a list of available movies, events, and other electronically recorded and stored types of entertainment, and select the one we want to see immediately or at a time in the future. In the same way, scientific, technical, vocational, or any other category of the enormous store of computerized information and knowledge can be called up on the television screen for our edification. In time, most of the libraries in the world and educational programs of many kinds will be available through telecomputing.

Legislative sessions and other meetings of government bodies open to the public can be seen live, with immediate viewer reaction and response possible if requested or allowed during the session. Or sessions can be recalled to the telecomputer screen from storage to review later. Banking and other financial affairs, payment of bills, and many business transactions and inquiries will be possible by computer. Products can be viewed, priced, and immediately ordered or put on hold for personal examination. Intercommunication will be possible among the hundreds of thousands of individuals and organizations interconnected in such interactive programs and services. There are no limits to the informational developments that can be foreseen and imagined for the future, including the speculative projections of George Orwell in his fictional book *1984.* The technology to accomplish them exists or is anticipated. The limits and rate of progress are those of cost and control, discussed later in this chapter.

This informational transformation will occur slowly. The multiple interactive systems must be developed and installed, and telecomputers designed and manufactured. And there are the fundamental societal, governmental, business, and organizational questions to be answered and the problems to be resolved which are discussed in this book. Relatively few people will be able to afford telecomputing in the home at first. But the same rapid reduction in the cost of telecomputing can be expected as occurred in the technological development and manufacturing methods which produced the electronic mechanisms existing today. It may turn out that the savings achieved by the electronic transaction of business and governmental affairs warrants partial subsidization of telecomputer cost. It is reasonable to expect that in time the telecomputer will be as ubiquitous as the television set is today.

What will slow the growth of interrelated interactive telecomputing is the capability of people to understand and operate the system. Over one-half of the adult population of the United States cannot read, write, or otherwise articulate well enough to hold the kinds of jobs and perform in the occupations that come with the scientific and technological advances that have already been made and are to be expected in the future. Of those who have video cassette recorders attached to their television set, some 70% are reported to be unable to set the timing mechanism to record a program. Presumably, telecomputers and interactive programs will be designed to be as "user friendly" as possible. And as more and more human activities are organized for telecomputing, people will have to learn how to use the system or face living with a serious operational handicap. It is possible, as noted earlier in this book in a different connection, that at least for a period of years society is divided into "knows" and "know-nots" as well as into "haves" and "have-nots". The two groups may turn out to include many of the same people. These socioeconomic divisions of the population could present a serious challenge to democracy in the future, as the less advantaged react to the much smaller groups that have higher individual wealth and the particular knowledge that constitutes power in the world today.

Another problem to be resolved is the security of the interactive communication system. There will always be "intruders" and "hackers" who will seek to invade or disrupt computer systems out of spite, technical challenge, voyeurism, or some form of fraud or other illicit gain. A system composed of many networks—which previously operated as separate entities each with its own security—is more easily and completely compromised when the separate systems are interconnected as one multiple system.

> People see the glitter and the glamour of the information highway, but they don't see the risk. . . . The vast majority of people have never really bothered to think carefully about what they may have to lose and what exposure they are taking for themselves by connecting to a network.[8]

As networks are added to the "information highway" and it becomes larger, more all-encompassing, and societally significant, protecting the accuracy and reliability of collective facts and figures and the security of personal and private information becomes essential.

NATIONAL INFORMATION SYSTEM

So far in this book television has been discussed as it exists today in the United States. A number of questions have been raised concerning its operations. Present practices are discussed by the public, by those engaged in the television business, and by others connected or concerned with the mass media. Little attention has been paid to what could be: how TV can be improved and do more than provide entertainment, advertising, and other paid promotion. The federal government has recognized the need for more than purely commercial television by establishing and supporting the Public Broadcasting System (PBS) with its policy of public service. But PBS is a small operation compared with television employed for commercial purposes.

What is the function of television as the main means of communication in our society? Is it commercial gain primarily or are there public objectives and responsibilities as well as private entrepreneurial purposes? Both are important. But as the most crucial functional element in a society, communication must be guided by public rather than private policy unless government relinquishes its role as the primary directive force in the society. The interests of the community as a whole are more important than those of any one of its components. They are best served by a national information system with the express purpose of serving the general public interest. Television systems for commercial purposes should be separate and secondary in the societal priority. The present system of networks could modify their purpose, change accordingly, and evolve into the national communication system. Or more likely, they would continue as a system providing commercially sponsored entertainment of various kinds. The telecomputing "national information infrastructure" now being formed would include several important informational services not now provided, and improve and expand several others.

News

Television is the primary source of news for most Americans. In times of emergency it is the official source of information for the public at large, although radio and telephone communication are vital for those engaged in emergency operations. Local TV news coverage is now limited, concentrating on crime and other events that are emotionally enticing, a consequence of the continuous competition among TV stations for high audience ratings. Undramatic news is more likely covered by the press. In a democratic society, which requires an informed electorate that votes constructively, the selection of what is included in the time allocated for news broadcasts should be based on the public's "need to know". It should not focus on news with dramatic appeal or even on what interests most people at the moment, since these attributes change rapidly in large part according to what is shown on the television screen. Cable News Network (CNN) comes closest to this objective. With the assurances of operational integrity discussed later in this section, CNN or its equivalent could be part of the daily content of a national information system.

Information

Two categories of information are not now available on network television: information that increases public awareness and understanding in general (discussed here); and information that encourages public participation in matters significantly affecting the social welfare (discussed in the next section).

Legislation, rules, and regulations enacted by governmental bodies are of interest and concern to segments of the population. Some of these relate to almost everyone. For example, health, building, and land-use regulations affect homeowners, real estate developers, contractors, lending institutions, and others. Changes in interest rates and taxes affect everybody in one way or another, as do actions relating to traffic and transportation. Large layoffs of workers by private enterprises, recall of thousands of automobiles by manufacturers to correct deficiencies, or the announcement of important new products are examples of actions by business which many people would like to know about. Taken all together, decisions are being made constantly by public and private bodies which affect most of us. They are reported in the United States in certain sections of some newspapers, in newsletters, journals, and special reports that are read by relatively few people. Information of general interest and importance should be included in one of the TV programs of the national information system to call people's attention to actions, developments, and events which affect them but they are unlikely to know about until long after the fact, if ever.

Participation

The second category of information not now provided on television has to do with promoting public participation. For example, in a time of drought and severe water shortage it is important for the people affected to know how they can avoid needlessly wasting water, and make more effective use and conserve water in the home and in the office: benefiting themselves individually and their society collectively. This informational program would be repeated often enough to encourage continuation of prudent practices. Similarly, a TV program describing how to prepare for an impending tornado, earthquake, flood, or other natural disaster—and what to do afterwards, serves both the individual and society.

Specially designed TV programs can assist the populace in their everyday activities and in situations they are likely to encounter. How to drive safely and legally, what to do in case of accident, and combating auto theft is important information for the driving public. Programs on drunk driving and drug abuse can illustrate the dangers and consequences of such behavior. Explanation of local bus routes, schedules, and how to use the system helps those who do not have cars and recent residents who are not familiar with the service. When certain crimes increase—mugging, carjacking, or follow-home theft—precautionary measures and advisable reactive behavior can be communicated to people in the area affected. TV programs describing the history, customs, and beliefs of ethnic minorities and other distinct groups promote understanding by the majority of the population and may reduce tensions and animus. A corresponding explanation of how minority groups can adjust successfully and participate most productively in the existing environment serves them and the society of which they are part. When interactive telecomputing is in full force, such programs can be made available "on call" whenever someone wants to see them, but their occasional broadcast as part of public programming benefits the individual and the community.

In times of emergency, national telecomputing would be the definitive reporter of events, the "recorder of record", and the official broadcaster of emergency information and instructions. Dissemination of public information for many generally beneficial purposes should not depend on whether a private interest is willing and able to pay for the program and contribute TV time. It is a societal responsibility apart from competitive profit pressures which serves people individually and collectively, particularly those under eighteen years of age and in the formative stage of their lives, who constitute one-half of the world population and will shape the future more than any other group.

> With what's going on in our society—the changing nature of families, class differences, income disparity, less church attendance, deterioration of schools—the traditional social institutions are not responsive to the needs of youth. The media have come to fill a void in terms of shaping attitudes and opinions. TV and the movies have replaced church and schools in the sense of shaping the way kids are developing, in terms of presenting reality and the way things are supposed to be.[9]

Education

As noted previously, one-half of the adult population in the United States do not have the education or skill needed to perform satisfactorily in the types of jobs being created by advances in science and technology. Serious enough in itself, this fact is even more disturbing because there are no plans to make sure that most young people, who have not attended or have dropped out of high school and are otherwise disadvantaged, grow up employable. Our public education system as now constituted cannot cope with the large number of undereducated adults and young people who are receiving no education. According to the U.S. secretary of education, "American education is now at a turning point—one that requires us to reach beyond current programs and practices."[10] New means of education are required.

Educational programs on public television are one response, specifically designed for the undereducated adult and disadvantaged youth. They should be available to anyone willing and able to watch, as discussed under Communication and Education on p. 98. The possibilities of mass education by national network television have not been explored in the United States. We have network programs explaining how to rebuild an old house, how to make furniture and do carpentry, but we do not have programs that enable the viewer to acquire minimal general education or an acquired skill. A national information system can fill this void.

RESPONSIBILITY

> Public utilities function in the United States: as business organizations performing some public service and hence subject to special government regulation . . . supplying some commodity . . . to any or all members of a community, or of providing some service . . . where exercise of the calling involves some legal privilege or a natural or virtual monopoly.[11]

Telecommunications function as public utilities in the United States, regulated by the Federal Communications Commission. They constitute a public service supplying information in different forms not only to an entire nation, but to viewers, listeners, and readers around the world.

> With satellites beaming down literally hundreds of TV channels over whole continents and oceans, countries lose control over information crossing the borders—an unstoppable immigration of ideas, images, and culture.[12]

No other public utilities serve over 95% of the population, providing the information vital to the functioning of our society. There is no other "commodity" or "economic good" of comparable importance. We are considering the lifeblood of a nation and society. More than a public service, it is a societal necessity. Besides its role as the primary source of news and other information, television has become a means of debating, proposing, promoting, negotiating, and even resolving political issues and societal problems. It has become the fourth power of government. The chairman of the U.S. Joint Chiefs of Staff has advised younger officers of the following, that even in war when military requirements take precedence above all else:

> Once you've got all the forces moving and everything's been taken care of by the commanders, turn your attention to television. Because you can win the battle [but] lose the war if you don't handle the story right.[13]

All public utilities are obligated to supply the community with the service they provide. The service must be assured because the community cannot function without the water, electricity, gas, sewerage, waste disposal, or telephone system which public utilities supply. The service must meet prescribed standards of quality. Because these are monopolistic situations, appropriate returns on investment are determined by public utility commissions.

A telecommunications public utility is responsible for the selection and dissemination of information: the most vital product of all for the community. The quality of this service is measured by its availability in the quantity needed, its accuracy, and its content. There is certainly no question of quantity. With 500 channels anticipated, informational indigestion is more likely. The accuracy of telecommunication, however, must be beyond question, and the contents of its broadcasts of high quality. No system—certainly one as vast and complex as a national information system—can be completely accurate all the time. Inaccuracies and other errors will occur. If these are acknowledged and announced immediately, and steps are taken to avoid repetition, a reputation of reliability is established without any pretense of infallibility. Accuracy is everyone's responsibility in their work, but the final, official, and legal responsibility for TV rests with the individual or organization broadcasting the information over the airwaves. Responsibility for the security of the system against malicious disruption and illegal use rests in the same hands.

The content of the material that is broadcast by a national system is not determined by unrestrained competition among TV stations, calling for more and more emotional incitement in program content to attract viewers and advertising dollars. It is determined by what is in the general public interest, with broadcast time divided among news, general information and announcement, education, entertainment, and limited advertising.

News programs include events that should be brought to the attention of the public whether or not they are of immediate interest or current concern. They do not concentrate almost exclusively on local affairs with an emphasis on crime and other dramatic or emotional nearby events. They seek to provide viewers with the information that affects them personally, their families, community, and country—present and future. They may include local, regional, national, and international news depending on the situation.

Information reports actions and activities of local government, business, and other organizations and individuals that people want to know about because many of them will be affected by what transpires. *Announcements* have to do with actual or potentially serious situations which must be brought to the attention of people and require responsive action on their part. For example, restrictions on water usage during a shortage should be explained to consumers. The public should be informed concerning problems of waste disposal or resource conservation, and how they can be resolved. People need to know how best to protect themselves against violent storms, fires, floods, earthquakes, power outages, traffic mishaps, fraud, or neighborhood crime.

Education presents programs specifically created to attract and to enable the undereducated adult and the uneducated young to acquire the formal education or occupational skills required for employment. This is a paramount need which can only be met by doing what has not yet been done: using the educational potentialities of television to their fullest extent.

Entertainment would not emphasize violence, cruelty, explicit sex, and generally negative content. Programs would be included that are concerned with positive personal behavior, family life, good citizenship, and personal and societal values which advance civilization and society. They would be treated as realistically as the violent content now prevalent, but they would have to do with the positive rather than the negative aspects of society. There is always the question of how often and for how long should advertising interrupt entertainment, including the "self-advertising" which TV and radio stations introduce during the breaks between scheduled programs to repeatedly call attention to forthcoming presentations on the same station.

The ultimate responsibility for the performance of a public utility rests with whoever generates the service provided and controls how it operates. In the United States this is a combination of private enterprise as the generator and government as the regulator, or in some cases the government as both generator and regulator. For television, it is the owners of broadcast stations who decide what information they will transmit, subject to any relevant regulations imposed by the Federal Communications Commission that is charged with supervising their activities. Owners have great latitude in deciding what will and will not be broadcast, determined in large part by competition for advertising and other promotional revenues, with content devoted mainly to entertainment.

Questions concerning current practice have arisen because of the excessive violence on TV after years of gradual escalation. There is an increasing awareness of the pervasive role of TV as people observe its impact on political affairs and public issues, on people's attitudes and reactions, and directly or indirectly on most aspects of society. The prospect of an information "superhighway" and interactive telecomputing reinforces the conclusion that television is a dominant force because it is the nerve cord of mass communication for the nation. These facts have long been apparent to political, business, and other leaders in our society, but the power of television in their own affairs has prevented their publicly questioning the role and conduct of TV as a societal force.

When the existing situation is recognized by enough people and political concern is aroused, the ownership and operation of TV stations will be reviewed even more carefully and thoroughly by regulating agencies than other public utilities. Because television has become the fourth power of government, the owners of broadcasting stations must meet the highest standards of character, responsibility, and motivation. Retaining a license to broadcast should be contingent on maintaining these standards, including not engaging in or permitting the falsification, misrepresentation, or technical manipulation noted previously in this chapter. Failure to maintain these standards should require an immediate change in ownership or directive control, or immediate revocation of the broadcast license. The number of television stations and other elements of the communication system controlled by a single ownership should be limited. Large monopolies in television and computing are potentially more dangerous to democratic institutions than monopolies in other public services. The primary criterion of monopoly should be the number of viewers and users directly affected: the total collective audience. No single person or organization should control the information transmitted to the entire telecomputer "audience" at any one time. No TV station should be licensed for the purposes of a single political party, a single business, religion, or any other substantive self-interest.

Competitive diversity in the public interest, rather than maximum private gain, should be the regulatory objective.

The owners of the mass media that will be integrated into an interactive system are well aware of the prospects the system presents for profit and power. Various combinations of television, telephone, moving picture, computer, and other organizations are exploring ways of combining to capture large segments of the enormous market for information, entertainment, services, and interactive communication which is forthcoming. Ownership standards and monopoly restrictions for the coming interactive communication system should be firmly established during the formative period now under way.

Requirements established for the telecomputing system by the Federal Communications Commission and any others adopted voluntarily by the owners and operators of the mass media themselves should be readily available for public inspection. A shorter version should be prepared, eliminating technical and engineering specifications and concentrating on standards of conduct, programming, content, and other requirements of direct interest and concern to the public. This smaller publication—clearly written in plain English—should be issued separately and distributed far and wide to those who use telecomputing, so that they know whether the system is following established guidelines.

EFFECTUATION

It is not only appropriate but societally essential that the mass media as they now exist, and telecommunications as they will exist in the future, are treated as public utilities. Communication systems which enable societies to function are more crucial than the service supplied by any other public utility. Because the mass media determine in large part what transpires in a society, they must operate in the general public interest as much or more than the executive, legislative, and judicial branches of government. In a democratic society they have the additional role of critic and supporter of the activities of government and private enterprise.

The critical requirement is that government and private enterprise work together in determining the types and quality of the programs that are broadcast and the standards of operation that must be observed. Government has the responsibility and legal authority to ensure that the mass communications function in ways that preserve democratic institutions, are competitive and not monopolistic, broadcast programs that are personally and societally rewarding, and meet national standards for program content and system operation. Private enterprise provides the incentive of potential profit, competitive initiative, and creative excellence. The mass media maintain a watchful eye on government and business. Together, government and private enterprise can accomplish what neither can achieve separately, but only if there is reasonableness and restraint on both sides.

For sixty years the Federal Communications Commission has acted for the national government in regulating communications as a public utility. It is empowered to issue and renew licenses for radio and television broadcast stations which "serve the public convenience, interest, and necessity," but is enjoined from "censoring programs or interfering with the right of free speech on the air."[14] The United States Criminal Code prohibits "utterance of obscene, indecent, or profane language." The role of the FCC must be expanded to cope with the growth in network and cable broadcasting which has taken place in recent years and is now occurring in telecommunications.

Few people advocate restricting the freedom of speech ensured by the first amendment of the U.S. Constitution to the point of not allowing any criticism of existing activities, institutions, and beliefs. But this does not mean that anyone can say anything they want under the pretext that there are no limits to what is allowed by the Constitution or is justified for some other reason. Freedom of speech is not a personal license permitting irresponsible or reprehensible expression. Throughout history there have been verbal and written expressions by individuals or small groups which brought immediate adverse reaction. Personal insults resulted in a duel or other conflict. False statements brought an apology or retraction, retaliation, conflict, or libel suits. Blasphemy produced retribution. Overt revolutionary statements led to confinement or imprisonment. Some of the unacceptable expressions voiced at the time turned out to be justified and accepted by the next generation. Most forbidden expressions were not prescient, and the relatively few that were do not nullify the need for societal restraints. Society determines at different times the extremes of expression it will tolerate that do not disrupt the community or threaten its survival.

Freedom of speech is a relative concept and term, balancing the desire of individuals to say whatever they like with what the family, group, or society will allow in their respective best interest. Individual expressions account for most of the advances that are made in the human condition, but unconstrained or misdirected expression by an individual can damage or even imperil the group or society. Restraints on freedom of speech may, therefore, prevent expressions that turn out later to be creatively significant, but this does not justify allowing a multitude of pronouncements that harm people and disrupt society. The relation between personal freedom of speech and the best interest of the society changes as the society evolves. This is the case today. At one time free speech was first expressed and localized within the immediate neighborhood or surrounding community, and gradually communicated to more and more people depending on its appeal and circumstances. Modern communications allow no such process of gradual filtration and spread. Individual expressions can reach millions of people and cause them to react in a moment of time.

Is "freedom of speech" in television programs or in movies that are broadcast permissible if it induces behavior that disrupts social order? When is human behavior so uninhibited or language so foul that it influences younger TV viewers and radio listeners to ignore the efforts of parents to maintain higher standards in the home? How much broadcast time should an individual, group, or organization be able to buy to present or promote what it wants? Such questions illustrate those that must be asked and answered because of the nature of telecommunication and its pervasive effect on people's attitudes and actions. Are the kinds of programs broadcast best determined by TV and radio station owners and program producers? Do audience ratings indicate what a population wants, and what it believes are in the best interest of the society over time? Is entertainment or some other immediate gratification the supreme human concern? If so, must representative government accept current wants as the primary determinant of its actions?

As a long-established independent government agency, the Federal Communications Commission is in the best position to address the many questions concerning the mass media raised in this book. They must be answered sooner or later. It is not only appropriate but incumbent upon the FCC to stimulate consideration of the basic issues involved in communications and seek information and answers from many sources, including studies and surveys of its own. Some important questions will not be resolved for some time. In the meantime, the FCC must act according to its own best judgment, in compliance with pertinent decisions of the supreme court and relevant legislation by Congress. To meet regulatory responsibilities in the age of communication and information now upon us, the FCC should be expanded and vitalized.

The substantive matters that must be considered are so fundamental and far-reaching that indirect representation of the major interests in communications is desirable. To achieve this, Congress could require that one of the following major interests in communication is a designated concern and competence of one of the seven FCC commissioners: (1) the mass media, (2) business in general, (3) the public at large, (4) society as a continuing entity, (5) political, legislative, and judicial concerns, (6) audience and user response, and (7) international considerations. The president would be required to indicate for which of these designated concerns an appointment is made, and to maintain the designated representation in filling unexpired terms and reappointments. Congress would conduct its confirmation hearings accordingly. Terms of office should be long enough to support actions by commissioners for the longer range future that are not responsive to current interests or transitory opinion, with reappointment and reconfirmation permitted. Decisions should be by majority vote in meetings open to the public, except those concerned with personnel, national security, and any other matters requiring confidentiality. Staff studies and surveys taken by the agency should be available to those interested. Strict rules of ethical behavior should be adopted by the FCC commissioners to prevent any improper political influence or semblance of undue partiality of any kind. To the extent possible, due to differences between the terms and times of appointment of members of the commission and those for elected members of Congress, members of the same political party should hold no more of the seven seats on the commission than the percentage their party holds in Congress.

These moderate changes will not be easy to achieve because the interdependence among the powers-that-be in communication could produce political deadlock until public opinion forces consideration of key questions and follow-up action. Politicians know that their election, re-election, and reputation in office depends on television and to a lesser extent on radio more than any other factor. This dependence encourages TV and radio station owners to ignore questions concerning their operations and resist any change. Various interests and organizations maintain that any significant constraint or requirement imposed on TV or radio broadcasts violates "freedom of speech". And the Federal Communications Commission itself does not publicly acknowledge that the public utility it regulates has become the fourth power of governance, requiring a new set of obligations and responsibilities as well as standards and restraints. Nor does it appear that the FCC is ready to assume leadership in determining how the available broadcast time should be divided among entertainment, news, public information, education, and other program categories.

The most important elements in these dynamics of political and economic interdependence have so far been under-represented if not ignored: the best interests of the population as a whole, the welfare of the nation, and the future of our society.

REFERENCES

1. Robert King (writer), quoted in David Barry, "Screen Violence: It's Killing Us," *Harvard Magazine*, November-December, 1993, p. 43.

2. Ibid.

3. Barbara Hall (TV writer-producer), quoted in David Barry, 1. above, p. 41.

4. Edmund L. Andrews, "FCC Votes a $600,000 Fine Over 'Indecency,' " *The New York Times*, 18 December 1992, p. zA1.

5. Ron Slaby (Harvard Education Development Center), quoted in David Barry, 1. above, p. 40.

6. Richard A. Kerr, "Earthquake—or Earthquack," *Science*, 26 October 1990, p. 511.

7. Roger Cohen, "Calais Rumormongers Mirror a Demonic Time," *The New York Times*, 30 October 1992, p. A4z.

8. John Markoff, "A Dose of Computer Insecurity," *The New York Times*, 1 November 1993, p. zC1.

9. Paul Juarez (Department of Family Medicine, Martin Luther King Hospital, Los Angeles), quoted in David Barry, 1. above, pp. 41–42.

10. Richard W. Riley (U.S. Secretary of Education), quoted in Lynda Richardson, "Public Schools Are Failing Gifted Students, Study Says," *The New York Times*, 5 November 1993, p. A10z.

11. *Webster's New International Dictionary of the English Language* (Springfield: Merriam, 1960), Second Edition, p. 2005.

12. John Lippman, "The Global Village: How TV Is Transforming World Culture and Politics," *Los Angeles Times*, 20 October 1992, p. H-2.

13. General Colin L. Powell (Chairman, U.S. Joint Chiefs of Staff), quoted in Richard Atkinson, *Crusade, The Untold Story of the Persian Gulf War* (Boston: Houghton Mifflin, 1993), p. 161.

14. Federal Communications Commission, "Regulation of Wire and Radio Communication," *Information Bulletin*, 10 1/78, pp. 8, 9.

> *In too many important ways, we have allowed this great instrument [television], this resource, this weapon for good, to be squandered and cheapened. About this, the best among us hang their heads in embarassment, even shame. We should all be ashamed of what we have and have not done, measured against what we could do. . . .*
>
> *Our reputations have been reduced, our credibility cracked, justifiably. This has happened because too often for too long we have answered to the worst, not to the best, within ourselves and within our audience. We are less because of this. Our audience is less, and so is our country. . . .*
>
> *We've all gone Hollywood—we've succumbed to the Hollywoodization of the news—because we're afraid not to. . . . People* ***will*** *watch serious news, well-written and well-produced.*
>
> Dan Rather, quoted in
> Rick Du Brow, "'Murrow' Offers Reminder of Sad
> Decline of TV News" (*Los Angeles Times*, 15 June 1994)

5

Concerning the Future

> The simple fact is that in any great organization—government or what you will—responsibility has to be borne and the day-to-day decisions taken not by the mass of those involved but by tiny minorities of them, and sometimes even individuals, chosen from their midst. This is not primarily because the judgments of the mass would be necessarily inferior. . . . The primary reason for this sort of selection is the reality that a large mass of persons cannot, if only for purely physical and mechanical reasons, be organized in such a way that it could carry out a regular and systematic program of decision making. For this a smaller body is necessary. And since such a smaller body has to exist, what is wrong with trying to see to it that it is composed of those to whom might reasonably be attributed the highest qualifications for the exercise of this function?
>
> George F. Kennan, *Around the Cragged Hill, A Personal and Political Philosophy* (New York: Norton, 1993)

The previous portions of this book discussed the existing situation and what must be done if we are to use our information-communication system to benefit and preserve our society. We can optimize our use of the system if we have the will to act, to plan, and to make the necessary changes. It is a challenging task, to be sure, since it involves two fundamental factors in our society: rational analysis by Congress, and the mass media functioning in the overall societal interest. It is a crucial task, since the preservation of democracy may depend on whether our society can function effectively with our system of democratic institutions as it evolves and is confronted with new conditions and situations.

PLANNING

In the long run, it will be necessary as the years go by for our elected representatives to perform more rationally and effectively in the general public interest. Science and technology are structuring an ever more complex society. Its functioning depends on increasingly intricate systems of production, banking and finance, tax collection, social security, utility services, transportation and communication, and just about every other essential activity. Not only must they be planned initially, but their successful operation requires continuous planning and operational management at all times. Because of their technically delicate nature, they are subject to malfunction caused by unanticipated external events, random mishaps within the system, malicious disruption by hackers and malcontents, and illicit use for wrongful purposes. If the operation of any one of these systems is interrupted, repercussive effects are felt immediately by other segments of the community or by the entire society. As the different operational systems become more closely interrelated, more and more of them will use the same population database, social security numbers for individual identification, and incorporate into the system data obtained from insurance, financial, mortgage, medical, and other organizations maintaining information on individuals, groups, and various categories of the population. Tax obligations will be correlated with financial information, production systems with data concerning transportation and communication, utilities with different population categories, and other systems with whatever information affects their operations and planning.

Disruption in one system disrupts others. Poor performance or failure in one can cascade into partial or complete collapse of the multiple master system, causing a societal slowdown or breakdown. Municipalities make sure that electric generation stations, which power so many vital activities, are not shut down long enough to paralyze the community. Safeguards are taken within the community and local stations are connected with a regional power grid which can supply electricity in emergencies. Precautions are taken to ensure the continuous operation of other services that are crucial to the community. As separate systems interconnect into a larger national system, preventing failure of the larger interactive system becomes as critical for the entire nation as local systems are for the local community. A high order of planning is as essential to preventing partial or complete failure of systems serving the entire nation, as it is for public services in localities throughout the land.

Developments in the structure and operation of society will gradually compel legislative action based on rational analysis rather than political self-interest pure and simple as is most often the case today. Legislators can readily determine their political self-interests and most politic behavior because their constituency expresses its current feelings and desires frequently and directly. There is no comparable constituency that expresses the condition, desires, and needs of the nation as a whole, but there are intense pressures from special interests and their lobbyists. There are a few clear-cut consensuses among the public at large indicated by public opinion polls of various kinds or by a genuine outpouring of communications expressing a common concern—usually stated in very general terms. How to implement the consensus is left to our elected representatives, but responsive action does not usually begin until years after the public has expressed its insistence that something be done about a major problem, be it the rising debt, crime, hand guns, health care and costs, drug and alcohol addiction, or illegal immigration.

For legislators to consider national concerns as well as personal, partisan, or parochial interests, there must be some analytical basis for determining a priority of national needs and the probable consequences of different courses of action. As discussed in chapter 3, there is no simulation of the "state of the union" for this purpose, showing the most critical interrelationships among its major components. This serves as a factual reference for decision makers in government and private enterprise, and concerned people throughout the nation. It helps legislators explain and justify actions in the national rather than in immediate and local interests.

For most people, national problems and issues are vague and indeterminate, the subject of stand-off debates on television between "experts," opposing convictions expressed in the mass media, and pronouncements by those with causes and self-interests. Consensus among those involved is rarely reached in open debate. From this multiple exposure of opposing argument the body politic is supposed to be able to formulate a reasoned judgment. This cannot be done without some neutral statement of factual and analytical information as a background reference. A simplified version of the national simulation, clearly portrayed and widely available, could serve as a common denominator helpful in reaching conclusions. Considering the educational deficiencies of our present adult population, this would not now be feasible for many people, but the simulation would benefit society by improving the quality of legislative decisions.

As noted in chapter 3, many kinds of simulation are used for different operational purposes. Few have been developed and used for comprehensive planning purposes. This is changing as planning becomes ever more essential in the formulation and operation of complex organizations and activities, which can be simulated on the computer screen to indicate the effects of different actions and assumptions. Improvements in simulation will be a primary concern in research relating to the process of planning. The process is so universal that we have taken it for granted and have given it very little intellectual attention. When planning is more widely recognized as crucial to individual, organizational, and societal success and survival, it will be taught in graduate programs as a distinct intellectual discipline and occupation, or as part of public administration and business management. City planning will be part of public administration or taught in schools or urban and regional planning, corporate planning in business schools, and military planning in academies and war colleges and other special military educational programs.

Although the context and particular knowledge required for successful planning differs with different applications, the general process and procedure are the same, intuitively or deliberately applied as the case may be. This procedure will constitute the core curriculum and primary focus for research in graduate programs of education in planning. The eight steps involved can be simply stated as follows: (1) Information relevant to the project being planned must be available or obtained;

(2) Information is analyzed to simulate the functioning and state of the organism; (3) Conclusions are reached concerning its intrinsic capabilities, limitations, and potentialities; (4) Specific objectives and general policies are determined; (5) Plans to achieve them are formulated; (6) Means and methods of implementation are devised; (7) Plans are monitored continually while they are in effect; (8) They are adjusted, revised, or replaced when significant flaws are discovered or conditions require change.

Each of these steps involves a body of knowledge and particular techniques. Some of this content, such as mathematics and statistics, is employed in almost every field of inquiry and endeavor. Some was developed in other fields for their purposes, such as scientific sample surveys and different kinds of simulation. A third group is the product of business management, public administration, or civil and military operations. This body of knowledge includes organizational structure, personnel policies, program planning and budgeting, and critical path scheduling. All together, the eight steps incorporate a large aggregation of relevant knowledge, information, and experience which is correlated and applied for the purposes of planning. It is an integration of knowledge, technique, and procedure like no other.

Planning is expanding in the workplace as the significance of the process is recognized. Because it is a universal process, it has been more widely applied than specifically labeled. More and more positions now include the word "planning". They can range from executive positions in top management to supervisors on the assembly line and team leaders in employee discussion groups. As would be expected, planning positions are to be found in just about every kind of endeavor. Operations research, management science, systems analysis, and systems engineering are terms also used to describe the process of analysis and projection involved in planning. The place for planning in society, and the employment opportunities that come with this substantive and professional capability are assured, since it is a determinative part of human activities.

While we can point to an impressive list of accomplishments made possible by planning, we have not been able to successfully manage our collective affairs. Witness the list of super-serious problems confronting human society today: wars, armed conflict, violence and cruelty, civil disturbances, hunger, ignorance, environmental pollution, pandemics, addiction, inadequate shelter and health care, and other societal deficiencies and inequalities. Taking into account our positive qualities and impressive achievements does not diminish the seriousness of the existing situation. Unless present problems are reduced by positive actions, not only will they become worse but they could combine to cause societal catastrophe. Use of nuclear and bacteriological weapons in wars regularly occurring around the world could escalate into unprecedented mass death and destruction.

People do not yet recognize planning as a distinct operational activity, field of knowledge and research, educational concentration, and intellectual discipline. Even those who practice planning regularly in their work do not distinguish it intellectually from other aspects of their activity. This is changing. As more and more plans are required to resolve critical problems, to attain desired objectives, to manage complicated systems, to accomplish any number of human purposes, they are identified specifically and incorporated as a vital part of the ongoing activity.

In the 1992 U.S. presidential elections, all three candidates made much of their respective plans for economic recovery. Governmental plans in the United States are no longer falsely equated by opponents with Soviet five-year plans, implying that they are undemocratic and call for absolute centralized bureaucratic control. It is becoming apparent that modern industrialized societies—characterized by scientific methods and technologically advanced operating systems—cannot function successfully without organized planning at the top level of decision making. Private enterprise, the military services, and some civil bureaucracies recognized this fact long ago. But many businesses wait until a recession or some other setback force them to formulate and implement comprehensive plans to restore profitability. For those who fail, a formal plan of recovery must be filed and approved by a bankruptcy court before they can emerge from bankruptcy. Command, leadership, and planning have always been recognized as essential in military operations.

Slowly but surely people are becoming aware that comprehensive planning is a supremely important human activity, a primary determinant of our societal prospects and ultimately our survival as an animal species. As such it assumes an awesome significance, recognized and acted on by few individuals today. The absence of comprehensive planning and analytic management by legislatures at the three levels of our government is a clear indication that they do not yet acknowledge its importance. Or if they are aware of comprehensive planning, they are unwilling to practice it for political reasons.

The political situation for our lawmakers today has changed dramatically from what the founding fathers intended or could have imagined. Modern means of communication have made it possible for local electorates to immediately and continually contact their elected representatives in Washington, D.C. or in the state capitals. By mail, telegram, telephone, telefax, and computer network, millions of citizens can express their reactions, attitudes, opinions, and desires to any and all legislators. Massive outpourings can occur spontaneously or by calculated manipulation. The public is also surveyed regularly by opinion polls, radio talk-shows, and other ways of determining what people are thinking and wanting at the moment. As a consequence, legislatures are bound to the current opinions of their electorate which they believe they must follow or face retribution at the polls.

With interactive telecomputing it will be technically possible some day for the populace to vote directly on the issues now decided by their elected representatives. Instead of the legislators' votes being tallied electronically in the House of Representatives or State Assemblies, the votes of people throughout the nation or the state would be recorded and checked electronically, and the issue at hand decided by direct vote of the electorate. With such direct democracy, the role of the elected representative would be converting public judgment and decision into legislation, or writing rules and regulations for its implementation.

The founding fathers saw government as representative in a fundamentally different way. Voters voiced their opinions on issues and the performance of their elected representative face to face or by other contact when they returned home from brief sessions of the legislature. At that time legislators explained their actions in Washington, D.C. or the state capital to their constituency, and sharpened their perceptions of political attitudes at home. There was no constant pressure for them to act in this or that way, comparable to what exists today. They could act contrary to current opinion or the desires of their constituency, if they thought it was in the best interests of the local community or the nation as a whole. They were considered political representatives rather than mere translators of current public opinion into legislation and other governmental action.

The difference between these two methods of governance is clear. One presumes that the public at large can act wisely and responsibly on complex issues. The other assumes that there are detailed, specific, and technical matters that take time, thought, and particular knowledge the populace at large cannot and will not take the time and trouble to provide. There are also problems and issues that require abandoning some immediate desires in order to achieve results in the future. The body politic is often unwilling to acknowledge and consider longer range objectives which upon further thought they might agree were necessary or desirable.

The societal role of small advisory and regulatory bodies is rooted in the age-old concept of a council of elders, composed of the wisest and most experienced members of the community. They acted to preserve a culture and governance of the society which favored its welfare and survival. They were also a court of last resort to settle serious disputes and controversial issues.

This concept is reflected in three of our governmental mechanisms. Were it not for their size, the qualifications of their members, and their actions, legislatures could be considered councils of elected representatives chosen for their wisdom and experience to act in the best interests of the community. Supreme courts are judicial councils of last resort for issues that relate to our constitutional tradition and are not settled by other means. Public utility commissions provide the close and continuing scrutiny of monopolistic community services involving technical matters and a detailed review which the public at large is both unable and unwilling to provide. Special advisory committees established by Congress and state legislatures for various purposes are in effect consultative councils. Perhaps the closest analogy to the historical council of elders are the special commissions occasionally appointed by Congress to study and reach a decision on issues which Congress must accept or reject without modification. The modified Federal Communications Commission suggested in the previous chapter is a council of elders composed of members representing the major interests involved.

The American public is ambivalent about our present system of government. We cherish our ability to directly influence the actions of our elected representatives, and doubt whether any small group of our peers can act wisely and well in our behalf. We are reluctant to accept the fact that in today's world there are political choices too complicated or too technical for collective consideration and decision by the public at large. There are national issues and measures on local ballots that are so complex or require such special knowledge that the best educated person cannot cast an informed and intelligent vote, even after trying hard to understand the underlying considerations. Were direct democracy by mass communication to become our method of governance, successful planning would depend on whether the electorate was well enough informed to comprehend and act constructively on technically complicated matters without having to abbreviate or eliminate aspects of the subject up for vote that are essential for adequate understanding. Fundamental questions of democracy are involved. Is the direct vote of a majority of the electorate better and more democratic than that of individuals or small groups selected to make certain decisions? Or should the electorate make the basic policy decisions, and representative individuals and groups implement them?

TELECOMMUNICATION

If the national system of communication is to serve the public interest and societal needs in the future, it will provide the six services the mass media now provide, with additional responsibilities and requirements. *News programs* report those items, selected from the mass of material available, that inform the public concerning important local, regional, national, and international events and developments. *Investigative reporting* reveals notable failures and successes in the performance of government, private enterprise, and other elements of society. *Public information* advises people of current events, emergencies, and situations requiring or needing public attention, cooperation, participation, or understanding. *Entertainment* diverts, gives pleasure, and contributes to the contentment and edification of people and society. *Educational programs* enable viewers and listeners to acquire knowledge and occupational skills on their own with formal recognition upon completion of prescribed courses. *Interaction* makes possible telecomputing services and transactions among individuals, governmental bodies, businesses, and other organizations and activities.

Programs in each of these categories would have equal time during the twenty-four hours of broadcast time available every day and night. It would be difficult to justify allocating a disproportionate share of the available time to any one of the six categories because there is equal societal need for the others. Network policy would encourage competition among the categories while maintaining equal broadcast time. Advertising is limited to a portion of each broadcast hour. This limitation would include direct advertising promoting a product or service; indirect advertising camouflaged as something else or introduced surreptitiously; and announcements concerning forthcoming programs on the same station or network.

Advertisers must be prepared to verify claims disseminated by the mass media, and to publicly refute advertising revealed to be false or misleading. No advertiser can preempt more than the designated time allocated for all advertising during a broadcast hour. Program content and method of presentation would conform to those established for the mass media in general. With these new requirements, advertising rates would be established which maintain quality television production without extravagant salaries, unnecessary expenses, and other excess costs.

News Programs

As has always been the case in the reporting of news, those items that can be included in the broadcast time available are selected from the multitude of events and developments occurring at all times. Those that are selected represent a range of events which people want to know about and those it is important to call to the attention of the public. Producers of news programs are aware that the selection and treatment of news affect and create public reactions, attitudes, and actions. Not only is news responsive to people's needs and interests, it can influence them and engender societal forces which would not otherwise have existed or have attained such intensity. Were this not so, there would be no point in advertising that promotes an object or service, only advertising that is responsive to desires expressed in some other way.

News events are not reiterated because their highly emotional content and dramatic appeal may improve audience ratings, but because they retain their relative importance with respect to other news. Particular subjects or lead stories are not predominantly featured for prolonged periods of time until their emotional appeal is exhausted, to be replaced by another primary emphasis with equal emotional or dramatic appeal. Transitory emotional response is not the criterion for news worthiness. Accuracy is essential. News that is inaccurate, censored, or manipulated is not only harmful in itself, but people soon learn not to believe news reports and the value of current information in the conduct of human affairs is lost. As noted previously, in today's world of mass communication inaccuracies in news reporting can ruin the reputation of an individual or organization overnight. And retraction does not completely remove the residual effects of the mistaken or false allegation. Responsibility for accuracy and for delaying broadcast or publication of news until its reliability is confirmed rests with both the original sources and with those controlling the mass medium disseminating the news. The reporter can confidentially confirm his story and its source to the disseminator of the news. And the news broadcaster can demonstrate by daily journals and other records that a reasonable effort was made to check the accuracy of extraordinary or dubious news he transmits to many thousands or millions of people.

Investigative Reporting

As investigative reporters, the mass media are an essential element in the system of political checks and balances required in a democratic society. Newspapers are still the initial sources of most disclosures, transmitted worldwide by television, radio, and telecomputing. With the privilege of evaluating and disclosing comes the responsibility of reliability. Investigative reporters are people with the same positive and negative personal characteristics as the rest of us. But they have even less right than the ordinary person to express careless, unsupported, or even malicious information and conclusions which are broadcast far and wide to millions of people who are influenced by this misinformation. A way must be found of preventing unconfirmed allegations which can severely damage an individual or organization. It may be necessary in some cases for reporters to reveal their source in confidence to a local authority for confirmation, or to a reconstituted Federal Communications Commission in the case of allegations of national import. As part of maintaining the societal value of investigative reporting, laws preventing discrimination against "whistle-blowers" would be retained and strengthened, since it is largely through "insiders" that major inefficiencies, frauds, and criminal acts are discovered.

Public Information

Public information on network TV, other than news, has been limited to announcements and descriptive information during local emergencies. Some cable stations provide live broadcasts of the meetings of governmental bodies. There are, however, numerous operational and regulatory actions by governments and decisions and activities by business which are not normally reported in daily newspapers, on television, or on the radio. Because they affect many people in the community, they should be reported promptly to the viewing audience as a body of special information useful for most people at some time for some reason. Being usefully informed includes more than we learn from news programs.

There are also local and regional situations that merit public attention or call for cooperation or for active participation by the populace: a severe drought necessitating water conservation; problems of waste disposal and trash separation; fire hazards; traffic violations injuring people, burdening the community, and costing the taxpayer; crime prevention; drug and alcohol abuse; or neighborhood cleanliness. Social situations of this sort are not now covered by the mass media except as occasional news reports and stories. The community as a whole and its members individually would benefit if video programs treating such societal situations were produced and shown on television and in schools to inform people and affect their behavior with respect to each other, their neighborhood, and the community.

There are other opportunities to advance social understanding and promote constructive citizen participation. Television programs advising the populace of the different culture and customs of different groups of people in the community should reduce the adverse reactions, tensions, or antagonism caused by misunderstanding. Informing people how they can educate themselves on their own should encourage those for whom school is out of the question to become occupationally literate, or to learn a skill which should help them find employment, and for others to add to their knowledge in whatever way appeals to them. Or a program advising and warning people of the trickery, confidence games, shady deals, frauds, and other dishonest transactions regularly practiced by professional swindlers would save prospective victims from being cheated out of their savings and the severe emotional distress that accompanies such a loss.

Entertainment

For most people, the prime purpose and contribution of television is entertainment. At one time it was the sole concern of the TV industry in the United States, until the appetite of the public for news was discovered. News is now second to entertainment in programming. Entertainment is delivered in many ways: by TV programs written expressly for the medium, movies old and not so old, cartoons especially for children, talk shows, soap operas, athletic events, musical presentations. The major concern about televised entertainment is its effects on the viewpoint, values, and behavior of large segments of society, especially the young who are susceptible to attitudes and actions which many of them would question or reject as maturer persons. It also adversely affects adult members of society whose deportment and inclination is at the tipping point between the legally permissible and the socially unacceptable, between the potentially malicious and the criminal. Until it has been proven scientifically to their satisfaction, there are those who maintain that there is no relation between the violent behavior erupting throughout the United States and the violence depicted repeatedly on television, in comic books, and in video games. Since this relationship is not susceptible to scientific proof or disproof, should we deny circumstantial evidence and common sense and refuse to act on presumptive judgment?

Excessive violence and cruelty, rampant use of guns and other lethal weapons, adultery and promiscuous sex, and thoughtless self-indulgence promote such behavior among those without firm moral and socially constructive values imbued by family, religion, or another positive role model or affective identification. Competition for higher audience ratings fuels an escalation of emotionally charged material as audiences become inured to the current level of aberrant behavior portrayed on the television screen. There are few compensating programs presenting positive, lawful, restrained, unselfish, caring, or even virtuous aspects of individual life and social conduct. As discussed in the last chapter, freedoms of speech and behavior are not a license to engage in unrestrained self-indulgence and antisocial expression and action, based on the assumption that human society has an innate collective strength and wisdom which enable it not only to withstand any and all forces operating to its disadvantage, but to advance strengthened by the challenge. Civilization will move forward whatever we absorb or do.

Since everything we experience is educational in some way, entertainment on television adds to the store of knowledge of those of us who watch TV and affects our attitudes, beliefs, values, and consequently our actions. Children are most susceptible to educational influence by entertainment and other programs on television. At an early age they find it more difficult to separate fact from fiction, since they have had little experience in the real world to make the distinction. "The average American child has watched 5,000 hours of television even before entering school, and by graduation the total will be nearly 20,000 hours."[1] As adults we are also influenced consciously and unconsciously by what we see and hear on the TV screen, as we are by what we read in newspapers, in books and magazines, and hear on the radio. We are subject continuously to informational inputs from our immediate environment and the outside world by the mass media of communication. Television and interactive telecomputing are the most powerful means of mass communication. Combining the visual and the audible they affect us simultaneously through two of our primary senses. Because they simulate real life more closely than the press and radio, their mental and emotional impact is greater.

Educational Programs

Excellent descriptive programs have appeared on television in recent years, most frequently on the Public Broadcasting System. They have involved science; the humanities; arts; history; political, business, and military affairs; successful people; and other societally significant subjects. Most of these have presented the subject so attractively and explained it so clearly that many teachers are finding that video tapes—accompanied by remarks by the instructor or a question and answer period—are more effective in teaching than the traditional lecture. Video tapes are as transportable as textbooks, and most homes have a video tape or disk recorder. In the communication age of tomorrow every telecomputer will be able to display video tapes or disks, probably both. We have a unique opportunity and an obligation to make network television a major means of education because it reaches so many people.

> It really is the beginning of a new approach to learning. Our teachers are saying [the network] has revolutionized their teaching.[2]

It should be possible in the future for every telecomputer in the home, school, or special instructional center to call up on the screen any one of a number of "self-service" educational programs. Some would provide the education required for literacy or for immigrants to learn the English language. Some would teach occupational skills, or how to improve one's capability in one of the arts and sciences.

> Nearly half of adult Americans have such weak reading and math skills that they were unable to perform tasks any more difficult than filling out a bank deposit slip or locating an intersection on a street map.[3]
>
> One very likely . . . application for on-line services is job retraining. The unemployed auto worker or other transitional contributor can sit at home, be trained interactively, tested on-line, and qualified by an interested employer.[4]

General education programs would lead to a junior college or university degree, with measures of progress, repetition as required, tests, and examinations built into the "open university" system. Periodic meetings in small groups with an instructor could be incorporated live when feasible. Or meetings and discussion can take place on interactive television. Graduation could be televised providing a videotape or videodisk record of the occasion, including a picture of each graduating student, superior to the photographs of the event taken by parents and friends. Television-telecomputer students could take as long as they want to absorb or formally complete an educational program, since it would always be available day or night. Those wishing to deepen or expand their knowledge while attending school or university could supplement their formal classes with additional television education in the same subjects. Since education will be even more important in the future than it is now for employment, the conduct of personal affairs, and personal satisfaction, a national system of educational TV may be used by most of the population at some time in their lives.

There are those who insist that only live instructors in the flesh can establish personal contact, encourage, and successfully teach people. Live and lively instructors would conduct many of the educational programs available on network television, in the classroom on the screen but not in the same room as the students. Most teachers do not claim that they are the best available; teaching assistants conduct many college courses while the professor concentrates on research. The most knowledgeable people who are outstanding teachers would conduct televised education. The "best and the brightest" cannot be obtained for every school classroom, but they can for every educational TV program.

Most important is the fact that educational television could reach hundreds of thousands or millions of people at the same time, in their homes, at their offices after hours, or at special instructional centers. There are millions of people in the United States who will not attend or complete high school, much less a junior college or university. Another large group have had some education after high school but need or want more to be able to get a job, to add to their knowledge for any one of many reasons, or even be able to cope with the increasing complexity of daily affairs. The most disadvantaged are illiterate, with little respect or hope for education, members of low-income and broken families often on relief and subject to drug and alcohol abuse, and socially disruptive or illegal behavior. Education by the television and telecomputer is the only hope of reaching and animating this group to help themselves. At least for years to come they will not benefit from our traditional school and university system of education.

> Personal computers delivered reading-improvement courses over the Internet to about 100 low-income homes in a recent test. Nobody would take the classes when they were offered at night at nearby schools. But students, and many of their parents, signed up eagerly when offered the opportunity to take lessons on borrowed computers in the safety of their own homes.[5]

If authors, screenwriters, actors, artists, musicians, and producers can create award-winning films attracting millions of viewers, surely they can create educational programs which will entice, encourage, hold the attention, and maintain the effort of most prospective students. In addition to long-established methods and techniques of teaching, there are new means of graphical expression and image manipulation which add tremendously to the exposition and explanation of both simple and complex subjects.

Besides programs on network and cable TV, video games can be used for educational purposes. They intrigue children, stimulate adolescents, and entertain adults. In the United States in 1993, an estimated 57 million people visited their local video store. Some of their purchases or rentals were video games.

Feature films are being produced on videotape for release directly to video stores and television stations, bypassing movie theaters which traditionally have had the "first run" of new movies. An increasing number of programs of all kinds will be produced expressly for or made available first for the telecomputer screen, some free of charge, some pay-per-view.

We have barely begun to develop the educational potential of our means of mass communication.

Interaction

The term "interaction" describes what is occurring in two dimensions. Instead of just receiving and listening to a television set or radio, people can telecommunicate "vertically" back and forth with someone else by written or spoken words, and "horizontally" with many people and many different systems of communication. Information expands at an exponential rate through these two interactions. New dimensions have been added to human and automatic computerized intercommunication. Through his telecomputer in the home or with his lap-top computer an individual can communicate from almost any location with people and organizations around the world. He can do this directly through "bulletin boards", with databases and repositories of accumulated information, and with commercial sources providing "on-line" services.

No one knows today how many personal computers there are around the world. One estimate is 132 million in 1993. Additional millions are part of the operations of hundreds of thousands of organizations and institutions of all kinds. Internet, the electronic network created by the U.S. government in the 1960s for defense research purposes, has expanded to at least twenty million participants in fifty countries, with an estimated annual growth rate of 15%. These figures will multiply many times as people and organizations find it necessary or desirable to be part of what is now the most essential operational element in the conduct of human affairs. And as the unit cost of telecomputers decreases with the increasing number manufactured, and network interconnections become less expensive as their original cost is written off, we can look forward to a world with perhaps half its population linked in some way with a vast maze of electronic interaction. We are at the initial stage of the most rapidly developing technological advancement in the history of humankind.

The uses of interactive telecomputing are many, and will increase as time passes. Following up on its original purpose, Internet enables those engaged in research and other scholarly endeavors to communicate with each other concerning their work, to interact back and forth immediately and "in person" or in small groups, rather than through published papers, occasional professional meetings, and ordinary mail taking much longer with less likelihood of making as many diverse contacts as can be effected by bulletin board, "E-mail", and fax. Everyone on the network can tap most bibliographical resources at libraries and other repositories of information around the world. As never before, the accumulated knowledge in the minds of individuals and preserved in written, sound recorded, and photographic form is at hand. This availability accelerates the advance of human knowledge and disseminates it rapidly far and wide. Internet users can participate in discussions on almost any subject and in mutual support groups of many kinds, a social as well as an educational experience.

Local computer networks are used for educational purposes, linking students in many classrooms at different locations with each other and with outside sources of information, enabling teachers to improve education in the classroom and to assist students at home with their homework. Although there are technical and operational problems to be overcome and costs that must be reduced before telecomputer-aided education in schools is widespread:

> Researchers see classrooms in the future without walls, making possible collaborative study for some subjects, independent research for others . . . probably even a redressing of issues of equity between rich and poor and large and small [school] districts.[6]

Bulletin boards are used by more than thirteen million people, and are reported to be increasing in number 70% per year. Thousands of informational resources are available. For different areas of intellectual interest, academic fields, professions, occupations, avocations, hobbies, business and financial topics, governmental activities, rules, and regulations. And for different groups of people, including ham radio operators, aviators, firefighters, genealogists, physically disabled people, and any group that decides to establish electronic interconnection. "Menu boards" enable the user to select among different sources of information on a particular subject. Electronic bulletin boards are also used by businesses to help customers adjust or fix their products, monitor patients taking drugs, for mail orders, selling programs to combat computer "viruses", or to record employee complaints and suggestions. Another set of informational resources are available at a cost through commercial "in-line" services: newspapers and magazines, newsletters, financial reports, and encyclopedias. Interactive services include shopping by computer screen, games, travel assistance, and stock purchases.

Yet another use of interactive communications involves automatic exchanges among proliferating databases. For example, a missing item of information concerning the individuals included on a national mailing list can be obtained from another database that contains the desired information. Income information obtained from applications for mortgages, bank loans, credit rating, and other purposes can be used for all sorts of marketing, other commercial, and even fraudulent purposes. Government agencies can cross-reference information in different databases for regulatory or enforcement purposes. Such interactions can be programmed to operate automatically by computer without human intervention. With more and more databases "talking" to each other, it is difficult to determine how the individual privacy we have had in the past can be maintained in the future. Subject references can be integrated to good effect. For example, chemical and pharmaceutical research references could be correlated to suggest areas of further investigation. Relating data on crime with disciplines concerned with human behavior may suggest or confirm significant interrelationships between the two.

A flood of information is becoming available and being produced as computerized and interactive telecomputing progress. There is now far more information than most people with a telecomputer can comprehend and use. At present there are comparatively few people who have the technical knowledge, know-how, and perseverance to master the complications of obtaining access to many existing systems. Only one-quarter of U.S. households have computers today. This fraction will probably increase dramatically as new elements are incorporated in the primary telecommunication system, which most people will find they must or want to use. Much depends on how "user-friendly" the systems are made. Costs should come down as more telecomputers are manufactured and the installation cost of system interconnections are written off. It will be years before it is known which of the existing, proposed, and intended systems will function effectively separately and as part of an integrated group. And it will take time before it is known which systems telecomputer users will pay for and which they will not.

COMPETITION, CONFLICT, OR CHAOS

Powerful and wealthy corporations and individual entrepreneurs are combining organizations involved in different elements of mass communication and computing, jockeying for dominant positions in this most crucial societal activity which promises to be both lucrative and supremely influential.

> Some 1,100 television stations and 11,000 cable systems are about to start a game of poker. . . . The stakes? Nothing less than the balance of power in the television business.[7] The newsletter *Digital Media* recently compiled a list of just those alliances formed to foster interactive television; it went on for six pages of small print.[8]

Those gearing up to control the electronic superhighway maintain that unfettered competition in the marketplace will ensure the best outcome for everyone, including the producers of information, those using telecomputers, the nation, and society. In a no-holds-barred contest among private enterprises, entailing substantial risks because of market uncertainties which will not be clarified for years to come, the winner will be appropriately rewarded. The devil will confirm the inadequacies of the hindmost. And the nation and society will have the optimum resolution all things considered. This argument does not take into account the economic losses of the losers in the high-stakes contest; the consequences for society if no guidelines or standards for the telecommunication system are produced by the contest; and the operational, political, and economic power which will accrue to the winner.

No one can chart a precise path of development today for a system with many indeterminate elements which will not be effected for years. Time and the competitive marketplace will provide answers to some of the uncertainties. But general specifications for a primary telecommunication system can ensure that the result of the organizational maneuvering now under way will meet the needs of society, without smothering competitive initiative. Equal time for each of the six communication services noted in the previous section of this chapter will provide a desirable balance between news, investigative reporting, public information, entertainment, education, and interaction. With this arrangement competition cannot change the equal time provided for each of these categories, but it can win the maximum time allowed for any single producer of information within any one of each of the six services.

A set of responsibilities and restraints, discussed or noted in the previous chapter, are called for in the general public interest. Television and radio producers and broadcasters are responsible for the accuracy and content of the information they disseminate. Advertising including indirect, disguised, and self-advertising is concentrated in a fraction of the broadcast hour between successive programs. Reiteration of the same subject or event is limited. Audience reaction cannot be induced or created artificially. The original form of visual images, sound, or other content cannot be altered or manipulated technically to appear or sound differently than it actually occurred. Positive individual, family, and social behavior must be included in program selection and content. No single person or organization can occupy more than a designated percentage of broadcast time during a calendar year.

Such a set of parameters focuses the competitive initiative of private enterprise with respect to the proposed primary information system, which is treated as a public utility because it is potentially monopolistic, and structured to serve the general public interest because it is the most crucial element of society. Whether the Federal Communications Commission will organize itself and constructively shape the national information system now in process of development remains to be seen. It has given no indication of such an intent. Its present policy appears to be "let come what may" from undefined competition among private enterprises, indefinite market forces, and unformed public attitudes. Judging from its record of accomplishment, rather than looking ahead and leading, Congress reacts only to crises and acts long after the need is apparent and the opportunity to achieve the best results has passed. There are no political forces today that induce Congress to plan ahead, and its organizational structure discourages rather than encourages such motivation. The president is limited in what he can accomplish by executive order, national leadership, and getting Congress to act. These are the discouraging realities of the political leadership situation today.

DEMOCRATIC OR AUTOCRATIC PLANNING

The observations in this chapter have to do with planning in a democracy. Planning is a universal activity involved in all human activity. Personal freedom of speech and action are restrained to the extent necessary to protect the society from the political dangers inherent in undemocratic extremism. The body politic must be willing to forego some short-range benefits to attain longer range objectives. In an autocratic society or dictatorship, the purposes of planning are, of course, very different because they are directed toward achieving the aims of the individual or autocratic group controlling the society. These aims certainly include the planning required to retain absolute political control, with little or no regard for the rights, desires, or welfare of people except as these affect controlling the society.

Like science, mathematics, politics, management, and every field of knowledge or activity, planning is neither intrinsically good or bad, constructive or destructive, democratic or dictatorial. It is a process which can be employed for the best or worst of purposes, to benefit or to exterminate people. Whatever its use or purpose, its successful application depends on communication as does every human activity and element of society. No activity can occur unless the information required to conduct it has been communicated at some time in some way to those involved. No society can function without communication among its members.

BASIC CONSIDERATIONS

There are additional considerations to be borne in mind, more basic and more difficult to evaluate than those previously noted. Will we as human animals be able to accept and adjust to what is required for our societal welfare and our survival? At first this may seem far-out and of purely speculative interest, but we have learned in recent years that our future may depend on whether we can adapt to the physical, chemical, and biological realities of the world we inhabit. Are we altering the environment in which we exist sufficiently to threaten or even predetermine our eventual fate? As evolving human animals can we react and act in ways that favor our prospects? The answers to these questions, however speculative they may be, affect how we manage our affairs. How we proceed and what we can accomplish with respect to planning and with respect to the mass media relates to whether we choose short-range coping or longer range actions directed at affecting the future to the extent we can. One approach favors letting matters proceed on their own accord with the least possible intervention. The other would establish general goals and specific objectives, with policies adopted and programs drawn to achieve them.

Not long ago, we ignored the effects of human activities on our environment because we did not know any better at the time. In recent years scientific studies have revealed how delicately balanced is the ecological system of the world: intricate and complex beyond belief and probably beyond human comprehension. We may be irrevocably altering this ecological system by industrial activities disrupting the upper atmosphere which shields us from injurious solar radiation. Pesticides and other uses of chemicals are producing widespread and deeply penetrating pollution. In many countries, most of the population cannot afford any other fuel and are cutting down woodlands and every nearby tree for firewood: causing erosion, disrupting the ecology of the area, and altering the local and probably the regional climate. Clearing forests to produce agricultural or grazing land also affects the global climate.

Some people maintain that science and technology and human wisdom in general will enable us to keep well ahead of such basic problems. Lower cost conversion of sea water or effluent into potable water, new agricultural products and improved strains of existing food staples, and synthetic materials will provide water, food, and shelter for the growing population of the world. We can compensate for different conditions at the earth's surface brought about by man-induced changes in the earth's upper atmosphere. This could cause massive melting of the polar icecaps, raising the water level of the oceans and flooding coastal cities which house a large percentage of the world population and industrial capacity. New cities would be built on higher ground or on enormous platforms floating on the ocean if the extent of the melting and the ultimate rise in the water level of the oceans could not be determined for many years. Medical science will have found a way of neutralizing the devastating effects of pollution, diseases, and unhealthy conditions spread by human action and inaction. And if in the far distant future we cannot exist on earth, we will migrate to a community we have constructed in earth's outer space, on the moon, on another planet where we can look back at the planet which we have devastated and look forward to our return to earth if and when nature has restored an environment once again hospitable to humans. Underlying such hopeful convictions or unrealistic speculations, as the case may be, is the assumption that the human animal is supreme in its knowledge and its ability to adapt. We presume that we are the species destined by universal creation to survive and prosper whatever occurs. If not exactly as we are today, in some interim or improved bodily and mental form.

That science and technology have been advancing at an extraordinary rate for many years is irrefutable. Discoveries, developments, and improvements of every kind are occurring at such a rate that the question arises whether people can adjust to the changes under way in the workplace, home, community, and closely interconnected world in time to prevent resentment and antagonisms toward the technocratic forces imposing change. By their nature technical systems require a high order of planning. They are the result of carefully worked out processes of development that are thoughtful, rational, and analytical. They require exceptional knowledge not only for their conceptualization, design, and construction, but also for their overall management, daily operation, maintenance, and continual review and readjustment in order to function at optimum efficiency. They require an alertness and unflagging attention which is not needed in less advanced human activities. They are by definition and in fact at the cutting edge of applied knowledge, very different from the usual and the ordinary we are accustomed to. Collectively, they call for successive changes in existing norms and preferences.

These features of scientific and technological advance reflect the characteristics of those who create and operate them. This small group of the total human population is like the rest of us in many respects, but they are also different in ways which set them apart. They are well educated and skilled. Their approach and their thinking is rational and analytical; it is oriented toward the future, toward improvement of whatever they are engaged in. They are accustomed to the continual change that is inherent and inevitable in their work. The motivation to learn, to progress, to acquire new knowledge and produce new results is strong. They would like to contribute to their field of inquiry, to the larger community where their work may be applied, or to the entire world of knowledge should their work be of such significance.

As scientific and technical knowledge expand and deepen, individual scientists can comprehend and keep up with a smaller and smaller, and a more specialized segment of the rapidly growing body of knowledge. To investigate some subjects they must work with someone else, as a member of a team, or one of a larger group of collaborators. There are special notations or languages that many areas of science and engineering have developed as a means of intellectual expression, of maintaining a consistent record of work done, facilitating communication among the group of concerned people, and passing on knowledge to future generations. Mathematics is the prime example, used by almost every field of endeavor and by those of the general population who have learned this special language. In some cases, it can be so esoteric that not more than a dozen or so super-specialists in the world can comprehend each other.

Every human is different, and there have always been people standing out from others because of their exceptional knowledge rather than dominant physical strength: leaders of primitive groups, tribal elders, shamans, priests, and scientists today. But the consequences of the unusual knowledge of such outstanding people in the past was nowhere near as impactful and far-reaching for their society as those of scientists and engineers are for ours today. Besides the pervasive effects of their knowledge on all aspects of our society, the numbers affected are much greater today than in times past. There are more than five times as many people in the world today as there were in 1800, and over twice as many as only forty years ago.

All of us began our evolution as Homo sapiens several hundred thousand years ago, a minute period in the billions of years during which animate life was created. Around fifteen thousand years ago, we ceased being primitive hunters and gatherers living in caves and rock shelters and began to select our living sites and construct our shelter. Farming and forming communities of people came later. We have been able to record our history and accumulated knowledge in written form for only a few thousand years. During this short time remarkable advances have been made in human knowledge and recorded for future use. During the past four or five hundred years the surge in scientific knowledge and technological development has compounded into the awesome accomplishments of recent years.

A form of mutation is occurring within the human population. The relatively small group of scientists, engineers, and other skilled persons responsible for technological advances is developing and progressing in power and prestige faster than the rest of us. The vast majority of people are different in significant ways from the small group who are shaping civilization and society. We share the same basic characteristics as human animals, but our respective sublimation of our primitive instincts is different. We are less educated, with less and less understanding of the complex technical systems which we must use to conduct our daily affairs.

Immediate needs and current desires dominate our reactions and actions. Often we react emotionally rather than thoughtfully and analytically. With a few exceptions, we are more concerned with the here and now than we are of the future. We are skeptical of the new and untried, resistant to change, most comfortable with the existing state of affairs. Planning beyond the needs of the moment is indefinite and risky. Unpleasant and disturbing realities are hard for us to accept, since they impinge on our hard-won satisfactions and real or imagined hopes. Illusions are an essential part of our coping with the vicissitudes of the real world, and retaining our hope that things will get better.

Instinctual drives inherited from our evolutionary and primitive past lurk beneath the surface, not yet sublimated to less emotional and more thoughtful responses. We harbor prejudices we prefer not to acknowledge, and look for scapegoats we can blame for our own inadequacies or failed hopes. We are subject to being caught up in the uncontrolled behavior of crowds, even episodes of mass hysteria. Aggressive attitudes are built into us because they have contributed to our evolutionary survival. Violence is acceptable or at least excusable behavior for many people. Our sexual drive and the breakdown of prohibitions against early sex is producing unwed mothers and irresponsible fathers at an unprecedented rate, with far-reaching societal consequences. In the present era of mass communication, we tend to identify ourselves with role models outside the family, adopting their attitudes and behavior.

Few individuals exhibit all these characteristics, but most of us have enough of them to typify the vast majority of the human population. This majority is younger than the scientific and technical group and the political leaders who are shaping our future. The differences that have always existed between the young and their elders must be added to those that have been created and intensified by the technological revolution now occurring throughout most of the world. These differences pose serious problems for societal stability as young people become disillusioned and resentful of those controlling the basic circumstances of their life and profiting in money and power from technological attainments. Disaffection is promoted by the regular portrayal on TV of the enviable life styles of the "rich and the famous", with few such programs on the poor and the unknown. The young are also abetted in their dissatisfaction by the frequent portrayal on television of the lengthening list of human rights, which are reported as desirable and attainable. But there is little or no exposition of the corollary of rights: the responsibilities which each person must fulfill if a democratic society is to function successfully and prosper. More and more of the young people under eighteen years of age, who now comprise almost one-half of the world population, have lethal weapons manufactured and distributed by many nations for profit and strategic purposes.

The world is undergoing greater change at a faster rate than ever before in human history. It has changed in almost a moment of time from a globe dominated by the Cold War confrontation between two superpowers, to one riven by tribal, ethnic, religious animosities, and regional conflict. The nations of the world, and groups of people identified more by cause than country, are more heavily armed with deadly and potentially devastating weapons than ever before. Human activities are affecting the balance of Nature: at the surface and underground, in the seas, and in the earth's upper atmosphere. World population continues to increase.

CRUCIAL DETERMINATIONS FOR THE FUTURE

Without decisive action by Congress, the serious problems confronting the nation today will worsen, producing a period of increasing social turmoil. The complex systems constituting our society will begin breaking down. With the prospect of societal disintegration, people will insist that something be done.

The inability of Congress to put partisan and parochial differences aside when it is time to act to resolve critical problems facing the nation is a serious weakness in representative government as it is now conducted. These problems cannot be resolved by adoption of the lowest common denominator of legislative agreement that can be devised among the many groups formed within Congress, each with its particular interest, political purpose, bargaining power, and insistence that certain self-proclaimed rights or substantive requirements be met before they are willing to participate in any overall collegial decision and action.

Except in time of war and real or perceived threat to national security, the public is reluctant to acknowledge the existence of problems which threaten the society, to accept the longer range commitments usually required for progress, perhaps to modify existing concepts, or to accept any proposal that incorporates an increase in taxes or foregoing an existing benefit. This would not be the case if Congress exercised collective leadership and functioned when necessary with "one voice", with few dissenters, to formulate, support, explain, and promote actions in the general public interest directed toward resolving the most serious societal problems. The public would be willing to accept such a unanimous expression of need, the conclusion concerning what must be done, and consequent decisions and actions: at least until what was done proved unsuccessful.

With such congressional unanimity and the support of the mass media, the re-election of almost all its members would not be threatened because of an unsuccessful effort in the past, without regard to the necessity or merits of the actions taken at the time in the general public interest. This is the fear of elected representatives today when they can be tagged as the segment in Congress at fault, trumpeted by their political adversaries and the mass media always aware of the public desire for scapegoats.

Will Congress be unable to act effectively at this critical time? Will it, as it has on occasion in the past, defer to a special commission appointed to analyze the most controversial and important issues, and determine remedial actions which Congress must accept or reject without change? Might its members become so alarmed by the course of events and their precarious political future that they establish a planning office to conduct analytical studies which indicate what they can and should do? Can Congress act in the public interest so determined? Or does the Constitution of the United States as presently interpreted and the self-interests of fifty states prevent the federal actions required for problems and needs that are national in scope? Will the body politic acknowledge distressing realities and support the actions necessary to resolve them? Will the mass media provide the public with the information it needs to react constructively, and encourage positive action by Congress?

The response to these questions will indicate whether our society—as presently constituted and as it now functions—can cope with the changes continually brought about by scientific, technological, and other developments noted in this book. Can the nation function successfully without comprehensive planning at the legislative levels of government? In addition to the difficulties inherent in our system of self-government, do we inherit personal characteristics from our evolutionary past that prevent our reacting as rationally and acting as constructively as the operational systems of our society require?

It is becoming difficult and at times impossible for us to vote directly or to develop a political consensus on the increasingly complicated matters requiring special knowledge that are presented to us for determination. We find ourselves dependent on a segment of the population with the education and skills to understand and operate the technical systems which comprise a large part of industrialized societies today. The original intent was that our elected representatives would obtain the particular knowledge needed and conduct the analysis and planning required to make sound decisions in our behalf. What needs to be done for our legislators to fulfill this primary responsibility, which they are not doing today?

If neither the body politic nor our elected representatives can act to meet the realities of contemporary society, our political system must be adjusted to resolve this untenable situation. There will be those who suggest that a strong leader or small cohesive group can cut through the political deadlock, if delegated the necessary political authority. Procedures restricting some freedoms of individual action and mandating certain activities would be necessary for a time. Frustrated by its inability to perform as needed and politically opportunistic, Congress would be tempted to accept the premise that the restrictive governmental changes would be temporary, although history indicates otherwise. This is the critical point at which intractable problems threatening societal stability and survival of the nation as it exists at the time force a choice between proactive democratic changes or adoption of incipient autocratic procedures. The status quo cannot continue.

The explosive growth of the mass media of communication in recent years accounts in part for our political and governmental dilemma today. They have vastly increased our impact on legislative decisions by our vote, and by massive expressions of opinion communicated immediately and powerfully to our elected representatives. At the same time, we have allowed special interests to dominate the political scene in Washington, D.C. and in state capitals.

Television, radio, and telecomputing are emerging as the central nervous system and political lifeblood of our society, determining its functioning more than any other element. Television is the primary source of news, other information, and entertainment for the American public. In ways noted in this book, it influences the reactions of people to current events, issues, and governmental processes. It shapes our attitudes in many respects. It can induce congressional and presidential action by its treatment of the news and other programming. It can influence or determine the conclusions people reach and the priorities they set for many subjects. These capabilities are extended and deepened as television and telecomputing become part of every household, and technical developments magnify their impact.

Because television is the crucial element of governance, it must function in the best interest of the nation and society as a whole. Unrestrained competition among private entrepreneurial self-interests seeking maximum profit prevents consideration and resolution of critical problems threatening democratic society. Government ownership and operation "in the general public interest" leads eventually to the dead hand of governmental inefficiency and autocratic control. The present combination of private enterprise and governmental regulation as a public utility that provides an essential public service is discussed in chapter 4. Is it functioning effectively as the major artery of communication for the nation? Will it function effectively as part of the forthcoming "national information infrastructure"? Does it provide other services and fulfill other functions vital to society that are most successfully performed as part of a nationwide television and telecomputing system?

In fulfilling the reportive and investigative role accorded them in democratic societies, the mass media perform an essential function. Without the "fourth estate"—expanded nowadays to include radio, television, and telecomputer—gross inefficiencies, transgressions of many kinds, and various injustices would go largely unnoted and unchanged. Economic reality functioning through the marketplaces in a democratic society correct some of the misdeeds of private enterprise, but not those of government soon enough to prevent great societal damage or political catastrophe. With the increasing impact of the mass media brought about by technological advances, their role of reporting and evaluating has become so powerful and pervasive that as pointed out previously in this book they have become in fact the "fourth element" of democratic government.

As they now report and monitor the human scene, the mass media emphasize unmet needs and misdeeds, faults rather than virtues, destructive behavior more than constructive deportment, disruptive and illegal activities more than positive accomplishments under the law. To an extent this is justified because adverse behavior and events threaten societal norms. Since this adverse behavior challenges the standards societies establish to optimize their functioning and advance their prospects, they must be highlighted. Positive performances and accomplishments, however, present no challenge to society, although they may threaten unsuccessful competitors. More important in the treatment of news by the mass media is the fact that negative situations are more "newsworthy" because they involve unusual, aberrant, or abnormal activities and events.

Emotionally stimulating news and disturbing investigative revelations are more enticing than news concerning laudable conduct and reports of positive achievement. Negative news attracts more people and produces the audience ratings that bring monetary profit, an enhanced reputation, and political power.

Also involved in the mass attraction of negative news is our psychological tendency to envy the real or imagined advantage or superiority of a brother or sister in childhood, an acquaintance in adolescence, or a co-worker or rival in adult life. Human life is competitive: with certain features and events in nature during our evolution, and most recently with members of our own species. Therefore, whether we are aware of it or not, we are attracted to news items that support our self-confidence or self-satisfaction by comparison with the misdeeds or failures of people we might envy. The mass media make use of this emotional attraction by accentuating the negative in human affairs, rather than the positive achievements which must predominate or the society would change character radically and eventually disintegrate.

This accentuation is contrary to the concept and practice of planning, which by definition deals positively with human affairs: setting objectives and determining how they can be achieved. Without positive support by the mass media of the importance of planning in the minds of the public, the necessity and the benefits of comprehensive planning by government will not be recognized. A policy that produces a balance of negative and positive reporting and evaluation must be adopted by the mass media if they are to fulfill their responsibilities as monitors of societal performance. At the present time, there is no published statement of responsibilities for the mass media of communication covering the many matters discussed in this book.

What can be undertaken and achieved in a democracy depends in large part, in one way or another, on how the mass media report and treat the subjects, people, organizations, and institutions involved. Whether and how we attain the political leadership and comprehensive planning required for democratic governments to perform successfully and survive, involves many things but depends on television more than any other single factor. This is one of the crucial determinations we must make concerning our future.

With the failure of legislative leadership in the United States, disinterest in planning on the part of the public, and mixed messages by the mass media, it is unlikely that representative government or the public at large will instigate needed changes for a long time to come. What is more likely to force the necessary determinations, the follow-up actions they call for, and the establishment of comprehensive planning as part of legislative government, are the changes brought about in the structure of society by science and technology noted at the beginning of this chapter.

Organizationally and operationally, industrial societies such as the United States are composed of distinct operating systems for different societal functions. Each of these systems requires a high order of planning in its initial design, current operation, and continuous maintenance. Together they constitute the integrated super-system that enables technical societies to function. If any component fails it not only renders everything connected with it inoperative, but also disrupts the multiple system of which it is a part. If it is not restored quickly the super-system is impaired. If several components breakdown, the society no longer operates effectively. Since no society can function for long without its operating stem in full working order, people in a democracy demand that it be fixed whatever it takes.

Autocratic rulers act to prevent any conditions that threaten the regime, and restore immediately any operational failures that could not be prevented. In a democracy these actions are more difficult and take longer because legislative leadership, mass communications, and comprehensive planning must function constructively in the general public interest. Whether organizational and operational imperatives force us to recognize our present condition, advance our prospects, and preserve our form of government remains to be seen.

REFERENCES

1. Paul Kennedy, "The American Prospect," *New York Review*, 4 March 1993, p. 48.

2. Connie Stout (Director, Texas Education Network), quoted in Suzanne Alexander, "The Digital Classroom," *The Wall Street Journal*, 15 November 1993, p. R17.

3. *The New York Times*, 16 September 1993, p. R7.

4. Tom Valoric (Editor, Telecommunications Magazine), "Carrying On-Line," *The Wall Street Journal*, 15 November 1993, p. R25.

5. Mary Lee Carnevale, "World-Wide Web," ibid., p. R7.

6. Suzanne Alexander, "The Digital Classroom." 2. above.

7. Elizabeth Jensen and Mark Robichaux, "Cable-TV Systems, Broadcasters to Play High-Stakes Game That Public May Lose," *The Wall Street Journal*, 15 June 1993, p. B1.

8. Stephen Kreider Yoder and G. Pascal Zachery, "Vague New World: Digital Media Business Takes Form as a Battle of Complex Alliances," 14 July 1993, *The Wall Street Journal*, p. A1.

> *At current birth and death rates . . . the world population will double in just 40 years, and will reach 27 billion by the end of the next century. . . .*
>
> *Growing at a rate of over 95 million people per year . . . the equivalent of adding a city the size of Los Angeles every two weeks. A country the size of Mexico every year. A country the size of the United States every three years.*
>
> *Over half the planet's population is under 18 and has not yet reached baby-bearing age. Ninety-five per cent of the current growth is in third-world countries with younger populations.*
>
> *The United States is growing a mere two million people a year not counting immigration. . . . However, each U.S. citizen consumes forty times more natural resources than a citizen of a third-world country.*
>
> Mark Winogrand
> *Dispatch*, January 1993

A sea change is coming in communications, information and entertainment. And in some measure it is already here.

The simplest way to understand the revolution is to first think of the personal computer and television set converging into one box. Now imagine the machine is interactive: Not only can you send text, sound and video, as well as receive it, but—because it is in digital form—you can manipulate and navigate through it pretty much instantaneously. . . .

Consumers, for instance, could have instant access to every movie and TV show and piece of music ever produced. They could get access to everything in the Library of Congress. They could go shopping with a sister in San Francisco, examining products in a "virtual mall" from all angles. They could order a driver's license. They could compare hotel rooms for a vacation. And they could exchange information with people anywhere in the world, about narrow topics they thought only they were interested in. And that's just the beginning.

Richard Turner
"Hollywired," Entertainment & Technology
(Special Report, *The Wall Street Journal*, 21 March 1994)

Selected Bibliography

Atkinson, Richard. *Crusade, the Untold Story of the Persian Gulf War.* Boston: Houghton Mifflin, 1993.

Auletta, Ken. "Raiding the Global Village." *New Yorker*, 2 August 1993.

———. "What Won't They Do?" *New Yorker*, 17 May 1993.

Barry, David. "Screen Violence: It's Killing Us." *Harvard Magazine*, November–December, 1993.

Berelson, Bernard. *Human Behavior.* Shorter Edition. New York: Harcourt, Brace, World, 1967.

Birnbaum, Jeffrey H. *The Lobbyists, How Influence Peddlers Get Their Way.* Time Books: Random House, 1992.

Branch, Melville C. *Comprehensive Planning, General Theory and Principles.* Pacific Palisades, CA: Palisades Publishers, 1983.

———. "Conceptualization in Business Planning and Decision Making, The Planning Control Room of the Ramo-Wooldridge Corporation." *Journal of the American Institute of Planners*, Spring 1957.

———. *Continuous City Planning, Integrating Municipal Management and City Planning.* New York: Wiley, 1981.

———. *The Corporate Planning Process.* New York: American Management Association, 1962.

———. *Planning and Human Survival.* New York: Praeger, 1992.

———. *Planning: Universal Process.* New York: Praeger, 1990.

Brown, Merrill. *How Americans Watch TV: A Nation of Grazers.* New York: CC Publishing, 1989.

Bullitt, Stimson. *To Be a Politician.* Garden City: Doubleday, 1959.

Communications, Computers, and Networks. *Scientific American*, Special Issue, September 1991.

Eastman, Tyler, Sidney W. Head, and Lewis Klein. *Broadcasting/Cable Programming, Strategies, and Practices.* Belmont, CA: Wadsworth, 1989.

Federal Communications Commission. "The FCC and Broadcasting." Information Bulletin, Mass Media Bureau Publication 8310-100, March 1993.

Friend, J. K., and W. N. Jessop. *Local Government and Strategic Choice.* London: Tavistock, 1969.

Gantz, Lt. Col. Kenneth, Editor. *The United States Air Force Report on the Ballistic Missile.* Garden City: Doubleday, 1958.

Greider, William. *Who Will Tell the People: The Betrayal of American Democracy.* New York: Simon & Schuster, 1992.

Halberstam, David. *The Powers That Be.* New York: Knopf, 1979.

Kennan, George F. *Around the Cragged Hill, A Personal and Political Philosophy.* New York: W. W. Norton, 1993.

Lichter, S. Robert, Linda S. Lichter, and Stanley Rothman. *Watching America: What Television Tells Us About Our Lives.* New York: Prentice Hall, 1991.

McCloughry, Air Vice-Marshal E. J. Kingston. *The Direction of War.* New York: Praeger, 1955.

McLuhan, Herbert Marshall. *Understanding Media, The Extensions of Man.* New York: McGraw-Hill, 1965.

"The New Tribalism, Defending Human Rights in an Age of Ethnic Conflict." *Los Angeles Times*, 8 June 1993.

O'Brian, Geoffrey. *The Phantom Empire.* New York: W. W. Norton, 1993.

Padella, Salvador M., Editor. *Tugwell's Thoughts on Planning.* San Juan: University of Puerto Rico Press, 1975.

Parcenti, Michael. *Make-Believe Media: The Politics of Entertainment.* New York: St. Martin's, 1992.

Steiner, George A., and Warren M. Cannon. *Multinational Corporate Planning.* New York: Macmillan, 1966.

Stevens, William K. "Humanity Confronts Its Handiwork: An Altered Planet." Science Times, *The New York Times*, 5 May 1992.

Stix, Gary. "Domesticating Cyberspace." *Scientific American*, August 1993.

Tugwell, Rexford G. "The Fourth Power." *Planning and Civic Comment*, Part II, April–June 1939.

———. "Implementing the General Interest." *Public Administration Review*, Autumn 1940.

———. "The Place of Planning in Society, With Special Reference to Puerto Rico." Technical Paper No. 7, *Puerto Rico Planning Board*, 1954.

———. "The Study of Planning as a Scientific Endeavor." *Fifieth Annual Report of the Michigan Academy of Science, Art, and Letters*, 1948.

———. "The Superpolitical." *Journal of Social Philosophy*, January 1940.

———. "The Utility of the Future in the Present." *Public Administration Review*, Winter 1948.

The Wall Street Journal. Special Reports. New York: Dow Jones: "Taking It Personally," 21 October 1991; "Group," 6 April 1992; "Hollywood", 26 March 1993; "Wired," 15 November 1993; "Hollywired," 21 March 1994.

Wallich, Paul. "Wire Pirates," *Scientific American*. March 1994.

Wilson, Edward O. "Is Humanity Suicidal?" *New York Times Magazine*, 30 May 1990.

Wilson, James Q. *Bureaucracy: What Government Agencies Do and Why They Do It*. New York: Basic Books, 1989.

Index

Name entries refer to the pages on which there is quoted material.

About the Author

MELVILLE C. BRANCH received the Distinguished Emeritus Award of the University of Southern California as Professor of Urban and Regional Planning in 1992. In the same year he was recognized as Distinguished Planning Educator by the Association of Collegiate Schools of Planning. In 1986, he received the National Planning Award for Distinguished Leadership of the American Planning Association. He has written over 70 professional papers, and is the author or editor of 19 books on various aspects and applications of planning.